THERE IS NO GRAY

THE BLACK AND WHITE TRUTH
ABOUT ADULTERY

MELANIE A. KAISER

WESTBOW
P R E S S®
A DIVISION OF THOMAS NELSON
& ZONDERVAN

This book is a work of non-fiction. Unless otherwise noted, the author
and the publisher make no explicit guarantees as to the accuracy of
the information contained in this book and in some cases, names
of people and places have been altered to protect their privacy.

WestBow Press books may be ordered through
booksellers or by contacting:

WestBow Press
A Division of Thomas Nelson & Zondervan
1663 Liberty Drive
Bloomington, IN 47403
www.westbowpress.com
844-714-3454

Because of the dynamic nature of the Internet, any web addresses or
links contained in this book may have changed since publication and may
no longer be valid. The views expressed in this work are solely those
of the author and do not necessarily reflect the views of the publisher,
and the publisher hereby disclaims any responsibility for them.

Any people depicted in stock imagery provided by Getty Images are
models, and such images are being used for illustrative purposes only.
Certain stock imagery © Getty Images.

ISBN: 978-1-6642-7832-5 (sc)
ISBN: 978-1-6642-7833-2 (hc)
ISBN: 978-1-6642-7831-8 (e)

Library of Congress Control Number: 2022917076

Print information available on the last page.

WestBow Press rev. date: 10/5/2022

CONTENTS

PREFACE

This is a book that I never would have thought I would write. Yet, four years and many sleepless nights later, it has become a reality. I clearly remember the January morning back in 2018 when I heard God speak very clearly to my spirit to write a book about my adultery. This was NOT a topic I wanted to share with the whole world. It was something in my past that I wanted to keep in my past. But I've learned that it's always best to obey God when He gives you an assignment, regardless how scary it may seem.

The best part about this whole experience is that I discovered a whole new level of intimacy with the Lord. Just when I thought I had reached the highest places I could ever walk with Him in this life, He showed me that there is *even more* than I can comprehend! This discovery has made the entire process worth every trial I had to face along the way.

My prayer for you is that this book will be just the beginning of your own personal and intimate walk with the Lord. Allow it to open your eyes to a relationship with Him that it so much greater than anything this world can offer. Let the words heal you in the places that you've never wanted to revisit and watch your heart be restored!

Love,
Melanie

ACKNOWLEDGEMENTS

Thank you to **Jesus Christ**, my Lord and Savior for saving a sinner like me! I don't know where I'd be without your love and grace. My life is forever marked by you.

Thank you to my husband **Scott** for your grace, forgiveness, love and support for this project. I know it has been hard to walk through this pain. I thank you for trusting me to share this story with integrity. I pray that we continue to press through every adversity we face, and I pray that our story helps others.

Thank you to my kids **Morgan, Anna, Sarah and Clay** for letting me tell the truth of this story. Simply being your mom carried me through the hardest days. You are my greatest gifts. **Anna**, I am a better person because of you.

Thank you to **Jana** for being my spiritual big sister. There aren't enough words to express what a treasure you are to me. You answered the call when you didn't have to, and I have been blessed by your friendship for over 30 years!

Thank you to **Carolyn** for being that friend that always spoke the truth in love. I know it wasn't easy. I am forever grateful.

Thank you to **Annaley** for being the very best accountability partner and friend. You motivate me to keep writing. You are an overcomer and am inspiration to me. You will tell your story one day, too.

Thank you to **Pastors Rob and Laura** for being my amazing pastors for 17 years. You helped heal a very broken young woman during my years under your leadership. And you taught me how to love people so well by the way you live a life poured out to others. Thank you for never allowing the size of your congregation to stop you from getting to know every person that wanted to be known by you and to know you. You have always exhibited Christ's love for "the least of these." Thank you for loving Anna, too.

Thank you to **Sandie**, my editor and friend. You are such a gift! Thank you for the hours you gave to help me with this project. I'm forever grateful for our many hours of conversation and your expertise in helping me.

Thank you to **Angel**. Your name is fitting, and you are an answer to prayer. Thank you for your wisdom, guidance, and commitment to stay the course. I have found safety to face the hard things. May God bless you for every hour that you have given to help another. I am certain that we will be friends in Heaven.

Thank you to **Tammy, Danielle, Terry and Veronica**. I met you at just the right time on this journey. Who would have ever thought that serving coffee, doughnuts, and (sometimes) breakfast tacos could be so meaningful. Our conversations have meant the world to me. You are the most fun, too. I'll take frozen custard with you any day!

Thank you to **Amber and Holly**. You are both a gift to me every day. I love our voice memo conversations. Thank you for being truthful and encouraging.

Thank you to every friend who has encouraged me to write my story. Thank you for allowing me a safe space to process this painful topic. There are too many names to name, but you know who you are. You are ALL important to me. My life is rich because of friends like you. I love you all!

PART ONE

THE SLIPPERY SLOPE

CHAPTER 1

✠ ✠ ✠

THE VOWS WE MAKE AND INTEND TO KEEP

Have you ever stood at the backside of a bad decision and wished that you could have a do-over? The old saying tells us that "hindsight is 20/20." In retrospect of a bad choice, we usually wish that we had done things differently, or at least paid attention to the warning signs.

I want to tell you about a decision that I wish I would have made much differently. Yet rather than dwell on what I can't change, I'm hoping that I can help someone else find healing from my mess. Even better, I may possibly spare someone from the inevitable pain in the first place. This was one of those less-than-ideal decisions that I am fortunate to say that God has redeemed. It was a defining moment.

Defining moments. Life is full of them. Pivotal points on our journey where we must decide which path we will choose. But not every path leads to a promising destination. These forks in the road require us to choose what we desire most, sometimes forfeiting the knowledge of a foreseeable outcome. Once the choice is made, a defining moment has happened. Eventually, we reach the destination of the path we chose. We will either be pleased with the destination or be completely remorseful that we didn't choose the other path. Either way, a moment has defined us by our own choice.

Fortunately, we don't have to be defined by a wrong choice *forever.* With God's grace and mercy, we *can* redefine our future. If we are willing to correct our navigation system, get off the wrong path and onto the right path, we have the freedom to decide what will be the outcome.

Some decisions leave lasting consequences that we must first face if we want to redefine our future. I am writing this book to share one of my own defining moments that sent me down a *wrong* path with some serious consequences, but how God gave me the chance to redefine my future. I am honored to have the opportunity to be transparent with you about how all of it happened. And I am humbled that God would use my story to help you.

As I look back over the years of my life to pinpoint when some major choices were made, I start this story with the year I believe I made THE most important decision of my whole life. My first big defining moment.

FUTURE DREAMS

The year was 1984. In my small town in Texas, pop music played on my boombox radio; prime-time television sitcoms, soap operas and game shows filled the network airwaves; stores were closed for shopping on Sundays, and most families went to church on Sundays-including mine. America was still considered a predominantly Christian nation. Most people got married in churches and used the same marriage vows in real-life weddings as on television.

I was 8 years old the summer of '84. It was the summer that I went to vacation bible school at Central Baptist Church. And it was the summer I gave my heart to Jesus, asking Him to be the Lord and Savior of my life. That vacation bible school at the Baptist church changed my life. It was a major defining moment for me that shaped the person that I have become. I knew that I was forever marked by God's love that warm day in June.

In my little small-town world, located in the middle of the Bible belt of the South, I grew up knowing that Jesus loved me, God was good all the time, and people stayed married *most* of the time. There were only a few kids in my class whose parents were divorced, but divorce was still viewed as a last resort to marital problems. And even though I was only 8 years old, I carried a strong conviction about the things I learned in church regarding marriage and the goodness of God.

In fact, in my make-believe playtime, when I made one Barbie doll marry a particular Ken doll, those two plastic dolls stayed married to each other in every future imaginary scenario I played with them. Like most little girls my age, I created many pretend wedding scenes where I, myself, was the beautiful Barbie bride marrying my handsome groom Ken. Make-believe was not only a fun game for me, but it was also where the idea for my perfect wedding of the future was formed.

Fast-forward to the year 2000. I remember our wedding day so clearly. It was a warm February day in Austin, with the sun shining brightly and the weather just absolutely perfect. That's what I love about this part of the country- we get nice little breaks from the cold for a day or two several times throughout the winter months. We took a chance that our wedding day might happen to be graced by one of these sunny winter days when we planned a February wedding. We were fortunate that our plan worked out for us. It seemed as if everything had aligned just perfectly for this special day.

We had the church, we had the big wedding party, we had the place filled with all our closest family and friends, and I had the perfect dress. On the surface, it looked just as picture-perfect as the make-believe, plastic doll wedding I had imagined as a young 8-year-old girl.

At the time, I sincerely thought that these details were all that really mattered- the way everything *looked* on the surface. Unfortunately, that perfect wedding dress, perfect venue and perfect weather were all covering up a massive tsunami that had been forming *below* the surface for years; and now, it was getting ready to create major destruction on the surface. As more and more undetected disturbances continued to take place, the threat of major destruction was imposing on our newly built life together, with two completely unsuspecting 'plastic' people unaware of the dire need to safeguard our marriage.

TSUNAMI- (Japanese: "harbour wave) also called seismic sea wave or tidal wave, catastrophic ocean wave, usually caused by a submarine earthquake, an underwater or coastal landslide, or a volcanic eruption.

(www.britannica.com)

PRIDE TAKES THE FALL

I don't think that anyone says to themselves on their wedding day, "Well, if it doesn't work out, I'll just commit adultery to meet my unmet needs." I would like to hope that most people enter marriage with the sincerest desire to live out the vows that they make to their spouse on that special day. I know that I never in a million years thought that I would one day betray my husband when I made those vows before God and all our family and friends on that beautiful February day. And I certainly know that the little girl who had played make-believe wedding those many years ago had the conviction planted deep in her heart to never do such a thing. Unfortunately, I got so wrapped up in the details of that one big day that I paid very little attention to the long-term life commitment that was to follow.

4

I can honestly say that adultery was the one thing that I swore I 'would *never* do' to the man I married. My pride led me to believe that I was somehow so 'above' such a terrible act that I was exempt from the need to safeguard my marriage from the idea. As a result of my pride, I ignored the warning signs of the imposing threat that was approaching. It was easier to stay 'plastic' and prideful than to admit that there was a problem bubbling under the surface. Sadly, pride is the very first lie that the enemy of our souls uses to cause us to let our guard down.

"First pride, then the crash- the bigger the ego, the harder the fall."
Proverbs 16:18 MSG

Pride is a very destructive thing. The moment that we adopt a spirit of pride in any area of our lives is the moment that we believe that we are somehow *not* in need of God's sovereignty over that area. It's the moment that we have just become our own god and denied the one true God to be the one and only Lord over our entire life. And most people don't even realize that they have just denied Him. The truth is that we *must* stay in a constant state of total surrender every single day in every single aspect of our lives to truly declare God as our one and only Lord.

"If any of you wants to be my follower, you must give up your own way, take up your cross daily, and follow me."
Luke 9:23 NLT

Jesus said to His disciples that, in order to be His follower, they must give up their own ways, take up their cross daily, and follow Him.

I admit that I really didn't grasp the gravity of this scripture for a very long time. Sure, I could say that I was a follower of Christ. But what I never really wanted to do was to surrender my entire life to Him, to completely give up my own way of doing things- *all* things- and die to my flesh and sinful nature every single day. Yet, that is exactly what Jesus has called us to do to be a true follower.

The question that most likely entered your mind when you just read that last paragraph is, "So, what *does* it mean to 'take up my cross daily' to truly follow Him?" Good question! It's the question I still ask myself every single day. I honestly believe that each person's journey is unique to him or her and that the answer to that question is one that you must ask God to reveal specifically to you. His truth is absolute, but each individual has a different place in their life where they still need to lay something down to Him. The struggle for one person may not be the same struggle for another. He will show you your own personal growth areas if you are willing to hear. Ask Him to show you what part of yourself you haven't given full authority to Him. What part of you do you recognize as being in opposition of His will for your life? It could be a blatant sin or something less obvious. I want to share what it looks like for me, with the hope that it will give you an idea of where to start.

VOWS AND COVENANT

When I stood on the altar on February 12, 2000, I stood before God and all our family and friends. I made vows- promises to my husband Scott and a covenant with God. Common marriage vows sound something like this:

"I, ____, take thee, ____, to be my wedded husband/wife, to have and to hold from this day forward, for better, for worse, for richer, for poorer, in sickness and in health, to love and to cherish, till death do us part, according to God's holy ordinance; and thereto I pledge thee my faith [or] pledge myself to you."
("Basic Protestant Vows" From Reverend Edward Searl, Unitarian Church of Hinsdale, IL. www.theknot.com)

Those were not just words intended to recite before a group of people, just for the sake of putting on a show in a pretty white dress that day. Those words spoke promises to another person with whom I was entering into a lifelong commitment, only to be ended by death.

There are no 'contingency clauses' to our marriage vows.

6

There are no 'contingency clauses' to our marriage vows like, "until he doesn't satisfy my needs," or "until he isn't physically attractive anymore," or "until someone better comes along," or "until our kids are grown and out of the house." You can fill in the blank with anything else that you may have said or thought for your own situation. The truth is that those vows were *for the rest of my life.*

A man "must leave his father and mother and is joined with his wife, and the two are united into one."
Genesis 2:24 NLT

I also made a covenant with God that day. And God takes covenants very seriously! When God makes covenant promises with us, He doesn't break them. We have a covenant promise in giving our lives to His son Jesus, which promises us an eternal life in Heaven with Him. God keeps His promises, and so must we.

"And the two are united into one. Since they are no longer two but one, let no one split apart what God has joined together."
Mark 10:8-9 NLT

&

"But because there is so much sexual immorality, each man should have his own wife, and each woman should have her own husband," and in verses 10-11 adds, "But for those who are married, I have a command that comes not from me, but from the Lord. A wife must not leave her husband. But if she does leave him, let her remain single or else be reconciled to him. And the husband must not leave his wife."
1 Corinthians 7:2, 10-11 NLT

Both the vows that I made on that day and the instructions for marriage in the Bible make it very clear that marriage is for life. God gives only two exceptions: one exception is if an unbelieving spouse chooses to leave a believing spouse and the other exception is for adultery.

"But I say that a man who divorces his wife, unless she has been unfaithful, causes her to commit adultery. And anyone who marries a divorced woman also commits adultery."
Matthew 5:32 NLT

In my case, my husband had not committed adultery- I had. I had made promises before God and people to be faithful and stay married until death separated us. And I had made those promises with the sincerest intention to keep them. It wasn't an issue of lack of sincerity at all. It wasn't an issue of understanding God's covenant and God's instructions for marriage, either.

The issue was that I didn't fully grasp an understanding of full surrender to God, the action of 'taking up my cross daily.' I didn't understand that to fully surrender also meant that I needed to allow God to work through all my past pain and hurts to heal them. Otherwise, they would continue to be the 'disturbances' I described as part of the tsunami that was building beneath the surface.

TAKING UP OUR CROSS

I don't claim to be a biblical scholar, so what I'm about to say is simply my interpretation and understanding of Luke 9:23 as it applies to my marriage. When Jesus picked up that cross to carry it to Calvary, he fully understood that he was about to give his life- his fleshly body- to death as a sacrifice for every sin ever committed, past and future. He completely surrendered to God's plan to save humanity. In the final hours before he was handed over to the Roman soldiers, he prayed, "Not my will, but yours be done." Jesus *was* and *is* the greatest example of what total surrender to God must look like.

"Not my will, but yours be done."
Luke 22:42 NIV

Just as Jesus surrendered to God's plan (will) to save humanity from sin, I must surrender to God's will for my life, which includes God's will for my marriage. And since God is very clear in His Word that marriage is for life, with only two exceptions, then I must

8

surrender every single struggle to His will- past AND present. I must surrender every hurt, every need, every expectation, and especially every temptation. By surrendering everything, I am placing them in God's control and trusting Him to work on my behalf. Anything with which I'm not willing to trust Him becomes an issue of self-sufficiency, which is a form of pride. And there you have it again: pride will take the fall!

There is no easier way. There is no better way. There is only *one* way, and that way is Jesus. Just as Jesus had to endure death on that cross to save us, we must learn that God's way for our marriage is the only way to save it. That's what "taking up our cross" looks like.

MARRIAGE: GOD'S DESIGN

I'm starting to understand this important truth, this *crucial* truth. My marriage, according to my own will and wanting things my way, will never succeed. I am not God. God created and designed marriage; therefore, God's way is the only successful way. And those vows are meant to be kept. Anything less than that will lead to some form of destruction, be it a tsunami that destroys everything in its path or an earthquake that literally splits you apart. Both are destructive. Both leave an aftermath that must be cleaned up. But neither are beyond God's grace and ability to restore.

There are plenty of ideas out there about the way that a marriage *should* look. New marriage 'experts' are coming on the scene and offering up their ideas for a successful marriage all the time. I've read numerous books, written with good intent, that claim to have found some new and innovative approach to a great marriage. But I assure you, the tried and true, infallible Word of God is the ONLY book that has withstood the test of time and proven effective. It goes without saying that the Bible needs to be *completely* read, *completely* understood, and *completely* put into action to be effective in our marriages.

I emphasized the word *completely* because it can't be a half-in/half-out approach when we are making those marriage vows in a covenant with God. Whether we have read God's Word in its entirety or not, by making that covenant, we are taking the responsibility upon ourselves to walk it out and live it. So, the first mistake we make is when we don't follow through with those vows by reading and knowing exactly what God says about marriage in the first place.

Sadly, this modern culture that we live in hardly takes the time to read *anything* in its entirety, much less the Holy Bible. So, it's no wonder that so many people fail to follow through with their marriage vows. We make promises based on words in a book that we've never read for ourselves and then we wonder why our best intentions fail.

> *We make promises based on words in a book that we've never read for ourselves and then we wonder why our best intentions fail.*

I was guilty of this very thing. While I grew up in church and learned God's Word in Sunday school, I had never really dug deep into God's Word concerning marriage, to fully comprehend what I was committing to on my wedding day. I can honestly say that I wholeheartedly intended to keep the vows I made. I was just ignorant to the fact that I really didn't grasp the gravity of those vows in the first place.

Without fully knowing and understanding God's desire for my marriage, those vows had been reduced to nothing more than a poetic piece of literature eloquently recited from an altar by a naïve young bride in a pretty white dress playing a part in a romantic storybook performance that February day.

> *Without fully knowing and understanding God's desire for my marriage, those vows had been reduced to nothing more than a poetic piece of literature eloquently recited from an altar by a naïve young bride in a pretty white dress playing a part in a romantic storybook performance that February day.*

DON'T OPEN THAT DOOR!

Ever since I was a little girl, I believe I have heard God speak to me in my spirit. Mostly, He has spoken to me to keep me safe from something or to encourage me, especially when I was very young. I can remember a very significant time I heard Him speak when I was 6 years old and living at our rental house on Taylor Street.

My parents moved quite a few times from one rental house to another when I was very young, until they finally bought their first home when I was 7 years old. I have a few memories of those first houses, and especially the house on Taylor Street. My friend, Tina, lived across the street. She had big sisters, who I always wished were my big sisters. I'm the oldest of my siblings and I always wanted a big brother or sister. Down the street on the corner lived Mrs. Fox. She was an older lady who also worked at the daycare that my siblings and I attended. Two doors down from us was the nice grandmotherly lady named Ms. Jody and her husband Harold. Ms. Jody was called the candy lady. She always came outside with a bowl of candy to share with the neighborhood kids. As far as I can remember, she was a nice lady who was harmless to anyone. That is, until one particular day...

I was sitting on the living room floor with my brother Chris, playing with some toys we were sharing. My mom was in the kitchen and my dad was in the bedroom. It was a day with moderate weather because mom had the front door open with the screen door locked and letting in fresh air. Outside the living room screens were honeysuckle bushes, blooming with the fresh fragrance of spring in the air. I loved that time of year when we could open the windows and turn off the furnace or air conditioner. I could hear the world going on outside our house and still enjoy the peaceful playtime in the living room with my brother.

Sometime during that afternoon, our playtime was abruptly interrupted by a very loud and urgent knock on the screen door. As I looked up from playing with my brother, I saw the nice neighbor Ms. Jody standing outside the screen door with a smile on her face. Just like any young trusting child would do, I jumped up with excitement to see her and began to walk to the door to eagerly let her in. However, just as I reached the door and stretched out my hand to unlock the screen door's hook lock, I heard an authoritative voice say to my spirit, "Don't open that door!! It's dangerous!" I stopped right where I was standing and hesitated for a moment, trying to figure out Who had just spoken to my spirit like that.

From the other side of the screen door, Ms. Jody became very agitated and spoke in a way that was very uneasy and somewhat scary to me, "Open the door. Just open the door!!" Her eyes looked wild, and her voice gave me chills.

Being the kid who tended to do what *I* wanted to do instead of what my parents told me to do, it was surprising to me that I didn't just open the door. Ya'll, I was NOT the kid who listened to adults when I should have! But something about that voice spoke to me with such authority that I didn't dare question it OR disobey it! So, I responded to Ms. Jody by saying, "I need to go get my mom first."

At that response, Ms. Jody became very irate and started to shake the handle of the door and demand that I open it right away. I started to back away at the same moment that my mom came running into the room from a phone call in the kitchen; and she firmly said to Jody, "Go home."

With that, she slammed the big front door in her face and locked it. She ran to the bedroom and told my dad something. The next thing I knew, they were loading us up in our car to leave our house and neighborhood. As we passed Harold and Jody's house, I saw police officers pushing her head down into the back seat of the police car, and she was wearing what I now know was a strait jacket. At the time, I remember being very afraid and not understanding why her arms were bound up in that white fabric and why she was being shoved into that car. Or, even more confusing, why was the lady who had always been so nice to us being taken away by police officers?

Several months after that incident, I remember riding along in the front seat of my parents' car, in the middle of the two of them, taking Harold to the state psychiatric hospital to pick up Jody. The hospital building from which she came out had bars and screens on the outside. She was completely lethargic in the back seat next to Harold on that completely silent and awkward drive home that left me so confused. We never saw Ms. Jody outside of that house again. And we moved from Taylor Street some short time later.

Just a few months prior to writing about this, I asked my dad about that incident. I found out that Ms. Jody had a complete mental breakdown that day, and she tried to kill Harold for no apparent reason. After he managed to force her out of their house, lock the door and call the police, Jody came straight down to our house to possibly wreak further havoc on more unsuspecting people. Harold had called my mom right after he called the police, so she had come running from the phone right after I had approached the door.

I guess I really can't know for sure what may have happened that day if I would have opened that screen door, but I have no doubt that the voice I heard was the voice of God. He protected my family and I from imminent danger that day. I'm so thankful that I listened to Him long before I even understood that it *was* Him. I would definitely call that a good example of the beauty of child-like faith. There was an authority in that voice that kept me from even questioning the 'why' and caused me to simply obey. Obedience to God's voice kept me safe that day.

And, I think to myself this present day, "wow- I sure wish I would have simply obeyed Him in every future situation that He spoke to me after that!" Life may have been a little easier and a lot less regretful!

I wonder how many times He has said to all of us, "Don't open that door [to sin]. It's dangerous!" Yet, we completely ignore His caution and do it anyways. Because even though we may not hear Him audibly, we hear Him with our spiritual ears, meaning that we hear Him in our spirit. We ALL have a conscience that hears God's leading to one degree or another, and our spirit is acutely aware of sin, whether we want to admit it or not. It's programmed into our DNA to know right from wrong. We don't have to have some sort of spiritual superpower to hear God speak to us. We just need to *listen*.

> *I wonder how many times He has said to all of us, "Don't open that door [to sin]. It's dangerous!" Yet, we completely ignore His caution and do it anyways.*

But no need to carry on about the would-haves/ could-haves/ should-haves regarding past "Don't open that door" moments. Instead, let's focus on the 'what-we-can-do-from-this-point-forwards.' We WILL have plenty of opportunities in the future to hear God speak to us and make the choice to obey.

I think that I have learned more from looking back at that incident from my present-day point of view than I ever could have learned without this hindsight. It seems to be a popular idea for most people. Hollywood has even made some very successful box-office hit movies about people going back in time to fix a mistake or re-live their past a second time more successfully than the first time! So, I know I'm not alone in seeing the benefit of that possibility.

Although this concept is a popular idea, it's not reality. No one gets to *physically* go back and fix or change things. We don't get a do-over. All we can do is move forward, hopefully taking the knowledge that we have gained through experience, to the future that is constantly in front of us.

Throughout this book, I am going to do my best to use my personal experience and the knowledge that I have gained from it to bring further insight to both you and me. We can move forward to our futures together. So, jump on this life-story train with me and see if we can grow from the discoveries that we make along the way. I'm rooting for you, and I hope you're rooting for me!

REFLECTION QUESTIONS:

- What moments in your life have defined you? How have they shaped you into the person you have become?
- Do you have situations in your past that you wish you could have a do-over? Were they "don't open that door" moments? Are you ready to surrender those to God today?
- What is your belief about marriage? Do you believe it is for life?

✠ ✠ ✠

CHAPTER 2

THE PAST REARS ITS UGLY HEAD

JESUS SEES YOU

Have you ever asked God, "Do you see me, Lord?" Do you ever wonder if there's anyone in the whole universe who truly understands you and has seen everything you've ever walked through? I know that I have! I often go to the Lord and ask Him to show me exactly where He was during different places of pain in my life. Every time a memory comes to me, I ask Him to show me a picture of where He was when I walked through that moment/season. Every time I take the time to ask, He is so faithful to show me how He walked beside me through it. He has been this way with people since the beginning of time. The Bible is filled with stories of lost people to whom God revealed Himself. Let's look at a very well-known woman in scripture:

"Now early in the morning He [Jesus] came again into the temple, and all the people came to Him; and He sat down and taught them. Then the scribes and Pharisees brought to Him a woman caught in adultery. And when they had set her in the midst, they said to Him, "Teacher, this woman was caught in adultery, in the very act. Now Moses, in the law, commanded us that such should be stoned. But what do You say?" This they said, testing Him, that they might have something of which to accuse Him. But Jesus stooped down

and wrote on the ground with His finger, as though He did not hear.

So when they continued asking Him, He raised Himself up and said to them, "He who is without sin among you, let him throw a stone at her first." And again He stooped down and wrote on the ground. Then those who heard it, being convicted by their conscience, went out one by one, beginning with the oldest even to the last. And Jesus was left alone, and the woman standing in the midst.

When Jesus had raised Himself up and saw no one but the woman, He said to her, "Woman, where are those accusers of yours? Has no one condemned you?"

She said, "No one, Lord."

And Jesus said to her, "Neither do I condemn you; go and sin no more.""

John 8:2-11 NKJV

In John chapter 8, we meet the woman caught in the act of adultery. We never find out her name. She is simply referred to by the label of her sin. In my mind, I picture this scene unfolding something like this:

The teachers of the law are notified that there is a woman in the town who is involved in an adulterous act at that very moment. (I secretly wonder exactly *how* they knew this and what happened to the man involved). They immediately go to the place where they are told that they will find her and burst through the door of the home without even knocking. They rip her straight from the bed where they have found her insufficiently clothed and completely ashamed of her nakedness. They force her half-naked body out into the dirt street, dragging her along like she's nothing more than an animal, and they bring her to the temple where Jesus is teaching a crowd of people. They shove her face down in the dirt right in front of him and all the people, completely disrupting His teaching.

The religious leaders had no regard for the woman's dignity or for the comfort level of all the people who were gathered around Jesus. They just threw her in the center of the crowd, leaving her completely humiliated and full of shame as she gazed at Jesus. Then, they demand that she be stoned for her sin, according to the Law of Moses.

I can only imagine the fear that she must have felt knowing that she could be stoned to death right then and there. Her heart beating up into her throat and tears streaming down her dust-covered face, as she frantically tried to keep her exposed body covered with the small amount of clothing that she *did* manage to grab as she was forced out of the house. And now she stood face-to-face with the man she had only heard about in the conversations from the townspeople- the ones who looked down upon her with condemnation. The question running through her mind was would this man condemn her, too?

The religious leaders brought the woman to Jesus with one intention only that day- to cause Jesus to say something self-incriminating that would give them reason to press charges against Him. This particular day wasn't about the woman or her sin of adultery. The religious leaders' motive was less about upholding the Law of Moses and more about their own ill intentions. On this day, they only wanted to use this woman's sin as a means to trap Jesus in some way.

However, Jesus saw straight through their wrong motives and their religious 'performance.' He looked directly past them to this woman face down in the dirt in front of Him. And in that moment, the entire event became *completely* about her. Jesus focused solely on the woman, and He saw her as a *person* rather than an object of scorn. He saw her as more than just a 'filthy adulterous sinner' like the religious leaders saw her. Even before she had a chance to speak a single word, He already knew her story. He knew her past and what had led her to this place of sin in her life.

Jesus *saw* her, really *saw* her. He saw her heart. He saw her pain. He saw her sin. He saw her shame. And yet, he still loved her. He gave her grace first and foremost; and then, He commanded that she go and sin no more. His love and forgiveness led to her repentance. Grace and Truth saved her.

How many of us who have found ourselves entangled in this very sin have questioned what led us to this place?

The story of the adulterous woman leads me to wonder how many of us who have found ourselves entangled in this very sin have questioned what led us to this place. I know that I had to take a long look at my past leading up to my sin to uncover some deep wounds that had caused me to be willing to act upon something that I knew was very wrong. This process of digging deep has proven to be one of the hardest, yet most important parts, of finding true healing and redemption.

Just like the adulterous woman in scripture, Jesus met me in my shame, face down in the dirt, naked and exposed before him and everyone around me. And yet He let me know that above all else, He still loved me. And once I took hold of the love and grace that Jesus so freely gave me, it was from that love that I willingly chose to obey His command to repent from my sin. Jesus loves you, too, my friend. He wants to get down on his knees in the dirt of your mess and give you that same grace and forgiveness. Are you ready to accept it and repent?

REPENT/ REPENTANCE

1. Repent- to turn from sin and dedicate oneself to the amendment of one's life.
2. Repentance- the action or process of repenting especially for misdeeds or moral shortcomings.

(www.Merriam-webster.com)

We don't know the story of the adulterous woman's past, but it is safe to presume from the scripture that she, like you and I, was ashamed of her actions and knew that what she had been doing was wrong. We can fill in the blanks to her story with our own stories and be certain that she had carried things from her past into her current sinful situation. Yet, that fateful day of standing face-to-face with the loving eyes of the Messiah looking straight into her soul, full of grace for all that she had done, would change her life forever.

Like the adulterous woman, I too had a past that I carried into my marriage. Some people refer to our unhealed past as 'emotional baggage,' and the truth is that we ALL bring some sort of emotional baggage with us. My past baggage carried issues of insignificance, rejection, and abandonment into adulthood. On top of the past baggage, I had unrealistic "plastic people" expectations of marriage and a 'when /then' mindset.

> *Just like the adulterous woman in scripture, Jesus met me in my shame, face down in the dirt, naked and exposed before him and everyone around me. And yet He let me know that above all else, He still loved me.*

A WHEN/THEN MINDSET

My pastor once preached a message about 'When/Then People.' These people are people who apply this standard to their lives that says that "*When* -blank- happens, *then* I will be happy." But then, when the one thing on which they had placed their expectation for happiness happens, they realize that they are no more satisfied with life than they were before it had happened. As a result, they move forward to the next "When/Then" scenario, **certain** that *this* time they will find happiness.

This mindset becomes a pattern of constant discontentment because happiness is always fleeting. Happiness is not the same thing as *joy*. And looking for joy by creating temporary moments of happiness will never work. The reason is because joy- *true* joy- only comes from the Lord. Joy is much deeper than what is happening around us.

> "*The joy of the Lord is my strength.*"
> *Nehemiah 8:10 NIV*

With that explanation, I can give you a few examples of how I lived with this sort of mindset for about the first 12 years of my relationship with Scott, both before marriage and during it. The very first 'when/then' scenario I created in my mind- a scenario that I thought would bring happiness- was shortly after I came to live with him. We decided to live together before we were married because we had been dating long-distance and we wanted to see how well we would get along on a daily basis. I know *now* that this was one of the first very bad choices we both made that opened a door for the enemy to gain a foothold in our relationship. Living together outside of the covenant of marriage is a sin that God clearly warns us about, and I will talk more about it in just a bit.

Well, it didn't take long for our true colors to begin to show and the once perfectly behaved 'plastic' people who had a blissful long-distance relationship began to argue and fight constantly over everything. If it wasn't about the toothpaste tube, then it was about dishes left in the sink. And if it wasn't about socks left on the floor, it was about money being spent over the budget. In addition to our struggles as a couple, my then 4-year-old daughter Morgan was part of the package. As a result, he was adjusting to a child as well as a full-time live-in girlfriend.

Now, I'd like to point out an important fact about living together when we were not married. While society may say that it's all just fine and normal, it's not Biblical and it will create problems. It gives Satan a foothold into the relationship right from the start because it is not God's design. It is fornication. It plants a seed of sin in your relationship that will later become a weed. God loves you so much that He wants you to enter the marriage relationship with the correct foundation. He knows the damage that an unbiblical beginning will cause which is why He set the guidelines in the first place.

If this is part of your story, it's not too late to change the narrative. Just acknowledge before God that you have been wrong with your choices in your relationship and seek forgiveness. And most importantly- repent, which is to turn away from it. If it's in your past and you are married now, confess and seek forgiveness. That's what I have done, and it has closed that window to sin. If it's your present-day situation, you can correct it by moving apart and abstaining from sexual intimacy until you are married.

Besides the fact that our living together before marriage was wrong, we should have seen these early struggles as a need to seek premarital counseling; but instead, I decided that our fighting was just because we weren't married yet. I believed that 'when' we got married, 'then' we would be happy and wouldn't fight so much. It was definitely wishful thinking at its best!

This pattern of 'when/then' thinking continued for years. 'When' we have our first child together, 'then' we will be truly happy because we will have our *own* baby. 'When' our first baby Anna, who was born with a rare disability, starts developing normally, 'then' we won't be so stressed all the time from the piling medical bills and constant health concerns; and we can just be happy. 'When' he starts to make more money at his job, 'then' we can pay off the medical debt and stop fighting over money all the time. 'When' our third child is born and doesn't have a disability, 'then' we can just enjoy a healthy child and we will be happy. 'When' we move to a bigger house and have more room, 'then' we will be able to relax together with our growing family in a nice home in a nice neighborhood. And we will be truly happy. The list went on and on, with each temporary grab for happiness passing quickly and increasing the tsunami pressure below.

The problem with my 'when/then' mindset is that I placed my happiness on external things, rather than looking internally to where the real source of joy comes from- a personal relationship with Jesus. Sure, life would be full of temporary happy moments and exciting events; but those moments would never last forever. I had to find internal joy from the Lord, deep in my soul, to sustain me in the hard times.

Can you think of your own when/then situations? They are probably completely different that mine, but just as relevant. I encourage you to journal about them. Spend some time really digging deep to identify them. After you've written them out, release them through prayer. Give them to God and ask Him to replace them with His joy. You'll be glad you did!

MANIFESTATIONS OF AN UNHEALED PAST

Without a doubt, there were plenty of problems on the surface of our marriage that needed to be resolved; but deep inside my heart were much bigger issues that needed the emotional and spiritual healing only Jesus could give. These were the issues that I kept stuffed in my baggage, unwilling to open long enough to really allow Jesus to heal.

Like the woman caught in the act of adultery from scripture, Jesus looked right into *my* heart to everything inside that had molded me into who I had become. He saw the little girl who had dreamed of this life that I would grow up to live. The little girl with her Barbie dolls and 'plastic people' dreams. He saw all the hurts and pains that this little girl had endured along the way to adulthood.

Jesus knew that all of it had contributed to the bondage that held me captive for a long time. He wanted to set me free so that I could experience true joy that only came from Him. He also wanted to heal those areas of weakness that the enemy could attack or use to tempt me. And He wants to heal you, too!

I grew up as the oldest child of four in a two-parent home. I was raised going to church every week, and I had parents who had been raised going to church regularly. However, hidden inside our home were the curses of alcoholism and abuse. In the moments where nurturing and encouragement should have happened, I felt the wounds of emotional abandonment and rejection instead. I didn't feel truly nurtured when I needed it most. As my parents stayed focused on navigating through their own dysfunction, nurturing the children was not high on their radar.

This may not be your story at all. I am blessed to have many friends who grew up in loving, nurturing homes. It truly makes me happy to hear people share their stories of their great upbringing. If this is you, I pray that you will maintain a heart of gratitude for your parents. And as you continue reading, I hope that my story will resonate with you in a completely different yet personal way.

While there were real problems in my childhood home, I'm careful to make sure it doesn't sound like it was all bad all the time. I choose to stay focused on the positives. I believe that my parents did their best with what they possessed to encourage me and celebrate my strengths. They were certainly proud of my good grades and childhood accomplishments. I am very thankful for that. I'm just not certain that I ever understood how to develop into the person for which God created me.

Even though we went to church, I don't believe my parents fully understood how to cultivate a personal relationship with Jesus. Without this personal relationship, they couldn't know what they were missing in the first place. And I'm not certain that they knew *how* to be nurturing in the way that a child needs to be nurtured because they hadn't received that themselves. My adult self knows that, without their own personal relationship with Jesus, it was impossible for my parents to be able to instill in me the truth that I was God's daughter with purpose and calling. They also lacked the skills to be nurturing because they were too buried in their own baggage at the time to take notice of anyone else's needs around them. It was generational, and the pattern had to stop somewhere.

I want to acknowledge that there has been much redemption and healing in my family of origin since my younger days. Please know that I give my parents grace and forgiveness for everything, now. Please understand that broken people can only operate from their own extent of wholeness. And the best way to manage this deficiency as an adult is to acknowledge the dysfunction and work towards your own restoration. Forgiveness is the first step towards true healing!

Once I understood that my childhood was a myriad of generational curses that had to be broken off our family to change the trajectory for future generations, I knew that I stood at a pivotal point. I made the decision that those generational curses stopped with me. It was definitely a defining moment! If you have a similar story, you can also make the decision to start a new pattern for your own family today. Remember that YOU have the power to correct your navigation system.

Looking back, I see how my childhood experiences created a deep confusion in me that told me something was not right in my life; but I didn't understand the depths of how wrong everything was. I knew that my favorite tv sitcom families never acted the way I had witnessed real life; so I was aware of the fact that our family was deeply flawed in a way that I couldn't quite explain. Unfortunately, a child cannot easily articulate the confusion and the degree to which they experience pain. Subsequently, when those hurts surface in adulthood, the accompanying triggered behaviors and emotions will often manifest as if we are still that wounded child.

The two biggest beliefs about myself that were planted in my mind in childhood that have affected me the most have been the lies of insignificance and disregard. I have also battled a lot with the lies of rejection and emotional abandonment.

As a result of carrying these wrong beliefs about myself into adulthood, any time Scott's actions triggered those deep-rooted lies, my response was that of an extremely hurt and confused child all over again. It wasn't that he was doing anything *intentional* to hit those deep places, it was just that certain actions triggered those beliefs. And much like I did as a child, I retreated within myself. I put up walls to protect myself. And unfortunately, my husband was on the outside of those walls.

I will go into much more detail about this in a later chapter, to give examples of how these triggers would lead to emotional reactions that eventually led to bad decisions. It's so important to ask God to bring these triggers to the surface so that we can become aware of them and break free from the effects of them. Regardless of the nature of your childhood, we all have a belief system that we need to assess and acknowledge the possibility of triggers. I want you to begin to make a list of things that trigger an emotional response in you and hold onto it. It will be beneficial to your restorative journey.

UNREALISTIC EXPECTATIONS

"And I, Barbie, take you, Ken, to be my husband."

It all just sounds like innocent child's play; but for me, it was a longing in my childlike heart for a normal that did not exist in my home. I saw the picture of the family I wanted on my favorite television shows. I loved those 80's and 90's sitcoms that resolved every problem within the 30-minute timeslot that the show had for airtime. I loved the sappy music that played in the background while the parents sat on the edge of their child's bed and spoke the "perfect parent" words of affirmation and encouragement.

I was so impressionable at that age that I believed those shows were true examples of what happy families looked like. I was so hopeful that I could have a family like that one day. And there was certainly nothing wrong with hoping for that in my future! Being hopeful for my future came from having hope in the first place. And hope is a large part of having faith. Hebrews 11:1 (NKJV) tells us that:

"Faith is the substance of things hoped for, the evidence of things not [yet] seen."
Hebrews 11:1 NKJV

My faith may have been misplaced on a fantasy tv sitcom-like family of my own, one day. But what I *really* needed was faith for a family built on the foundation of God's Word. I didn't need to hold onto unrealistic expectations. I didn't need a plastic family. I didn't need a sitcom family. And I didn't need to bring the dysfunction of my past into my future family.

I would love to stop right here and tell you that I was the person that just dug right into my past hurts when they surfaced and that I faced them head-on with no hesitation. Boy, that would have made life a lot easier! At the time of all this surmounting mess, I wanted nothing to do with working on the issues below the surface, even though they were the cause of so many of my wrong choices. Those past issues were bubbling deep down, just like how a tsunami starts deep down on the ocean floor long before it ever wreaks its disastrous havoc on the surface.

I would love to tell you that I always recognized a trigger for what it truly was when Scott unintentionally acted in a way that hit me deep where it hurt the worst. I wish that I knew better than to put all that expectation on Scott to do things differently in the areas that I wasn't yet aware that they existed as triggers in the first place. And I wish that time could have just worked those issues out by themselves.

Unfortunately, unresolved issues don't just work out by themselves. I'm *still* unpacking the baggage and peeling back the layers, little by little. I'm certain that it's a lifetime process, which is why I'm so thankful that God promises us that:

"He who began a good work in you will carry it on to completion until the day of Christ Jesus."
Philippians 1:6 NIV

So, I will continue to press in and move forward. My hope for you is that you will be encouraged to do the same. Begin to think about your own unrealistic expectations and possible triggers. What about your unresolved issues? Start to dive into each of these topics as I address them. Be honest with yourself, too.

I wonder if this book may be your first attempt to find healing in your marriage or life in general. Or it may be the first time you have ever heard of any of these ideas, and you are just now coming into a place of deeper self-discovery. Maybe you still don't know why you picked up this book in the first place, but you're starting to see that you can relate to some of it in one way or another. Whatever the case may be, I am praying that it will lead you in the right direction. If anything, let it be a catalyst to start seeking your next step.

As you continue to self-reflect and seek answers, I invite you into a small portion of some of my own personally revealed causes of the alluding disaster that eventually followed my unresolved issues.

UNMET NEEDS

I want to start with this truth so that we don't forget it: God is the only one who can perfectly meet our needs. Not parents. Not grandparents. Not friends or siblings. No romantic relationship will ever give us complete and total fulfillment, either. Yes, we need people. But we need a personal relationship with our Father in Heaven more than all the above.

We will spare ourselves a lot of unnecessary pain by taking this one truth to heart and believing it. It will help us to avoid putting so much investment in trying to find that perfect person who we think will make us whole. The movie *Jerry Maguire* was wrong when Tom Cruise's character said to his separated wife, "You complete me." It sounds all romantic and such, but no one completes us except God.

If we take one too many ideologies from romantic movies and add them to all the things that we already expect from our flawed human spouse, we will come up short and disappointed every single time. Humans just cannot be for us what only God intended for Himself to be for us. God placed that longing in our hearts for only God himself to fill.

> *Humans just cannot be for us what only God intended for Himself to be for us. God placed that longing in our hearts for only God himself to fill.*

I *do* want to acknowledge that marriage was created by God for the purpose of two people coming together as one and for building a life together. After all, I told you before that God created marriage. And marriage was meant for an important purpose. Marriage is a representation of Christ's relationship to His church. We have needs that we bring to our marriage relationship. We want love and respect, support, partnership, friendship, physical affection, sex, help, a listening ear, a voice of encouragement, and many more.

When those needs don't get met, or get ignored altogether, both people suffer. Even if only one person in the relationship is the one feeling ignored and feeling like their needs aren't being met, it will affect the entire marriage.

My personal struggle was with feeling insignificant to Scott and feeling disregarded by Scott. For me, I felt most loved when I felt like an important part of his life, and I felt most unloved when I felt like my needs were ignored entirely. When I didn't feel supported or like an equal partner, it took me back to the same feelings I had as a child in a dysfunctional home. Over time, I began to view him the same way I had viewed my parents. Professionals call this "misplaced emotions." With each hurtful experience, I retreated further within myself until I was completely withdrawn and shut down.

I leave you with the following challenge: spend some quality quiet time praying for revelation as you answer the reflection questions below. Be honest with yourself and with God, and don't rush the process.

REFLECTION QUESTIONS:

- Identify your own needs in your life that you don't feel are being met. They don't have to be needs met by a specific person, just general unmet needs. After you've made the list, begin asking God to meet each need, listing them one at a time to Him. And trust Him to do it.
- If you believe that you have become withdrawn and shut down in certain parts of your heart, ask God to reveal them to you so that He can be invited to revive those places back to life. This step is crucial to the process. God wants your whole heart!

CHAPTER 3

✠ ✠ ✠

NO SUCH THING AS "FAKE IT 'TIL YOU MAKE IT"

In the last chapter, I mentioned the fact that I was placing my source of happiness in external things. And that the reality is that true joy and happiness do not come from external circumstances at all. So, even if I continued to see every one of my 'when/ then' scenarios come to pass, I was seeking joy and happiness from the wrong source. Romans 14:17 tells us:

> *"For the kingdom of God is not a matter of eating and drinking, but of righteousness, peace and joy in the Holy Spirit."*
> *Romans 14:17 NKJV*

What this means is that our joy must come from the Holy Spirit *within* us. There is not a single external scenario in this world that will bring the everlasting joy that we experience in the goodness of God. Joy is a fruit of the Holy Spirit. When He lives in us and reigns over our lives, the results that are produced are His fruit.

> *"But the Holy Spirit produces this kind of fruit in our lives: love, joy, peace, patience, kindness, goodness, faithfulness, gentleness, and self-control. There is no law against these things!"*
> *Galatians 5:22-23 NLT*

The real root of my problem didn't stem from a lack of finding the perfect marriage and family scenario. It stemmed from something much deeper, or dare I say, *many* somethings deeper in my heart and soul that had never been brought to the Great Physician God to be laid out before Him on the miraculous operating table of grace and mercy.

The lack of joy and happiness in my marriage came from a deep void in my soul where I was full of sadness and hurt. I had carried so much baggage from this void that I couldn't have possibly found joy and happiness in the most picture-perfect-plastic-people-All-American-Dream scenarios that ever existed- IF there really is one in the first place.

THE COST OF CHECKED BAGGAGE

My family doesn't fly often, but when we do, it is always quite an ordeal. In addition to the fact that we have 4 kids, our daughter Anna is disabled and in a wheelchair. Flying for us entails bringing along a lot of stuff. We have baggage to check, baggage for carry-on, Anna's special car seat to check, her wheelchair to go through special security to be able to take through the gate, special blankets, and stuffed animals to carry on, plus everything else that one of my other kids thinks they *need* to travel.

Needless to say, our goal is always to get as much of our stuff as possible to fit into as few of checked bags as possible so that we can drop them off as soon as we arrive at the airport, rather than tote it through the entire place with our traveling circus. We don't want to carry all that stuff and we certainly don't want to pay a massive fee for so many checked bags. It is always hard enough to go through ticketing and security with kids, bags, toys, and wheelchair in tote, plus race to our gate to be on time for our departure. Adding to that fiasco, it would be wasteful to spend more money on an abundance of checked baggage that would exceed the cost of an additional passenger ticket altogether.

However, we must be very careful about just how much stuff we stuff in our checked baggage because there is a weight limit. And believe it or not, we have exceeded the checked baggage weight limit in the past, being forced to open it up and let go of some of the items that we really didn't need to be bringing along in the first place.

As silly as this all sounds, the point of this story isn't about our bad vacationing over-packing problem. It's about that checked baggage weight limit and why all airlines must have one.

You see, in order to get that big jet airplane full of people and their stuff off the ground and safely into the air, there is a weight limit that the plane must stay below. If the airlines ignored this safety regulation and let everyone bring as much overstuffed baggage as they wanted onto the plane, it could lead to great disaster. The plane could fail to get off the ground at all, or worse, have maneuvering complications while in flight causing it to come crashing down. And something as simple as keeping a baggage weight limit helps prevent those risks. Interesting, isn't it?

If we would just apply the same baggage weight limit to our lives, just think of how many times we could avoid failed launches, unnecessary complications, and total crashes! Baggage seems like such a minor detail until we look at it with the viewpoint of an airplane, doesn't it?

I mentioned the idea of emotional baggage in the last chapter, and I would like to elaborate on it here. Baggage is a big deal. I define it as everything packed up in the suitcases of our hearts and souls, stuffed to the brim, and sometimes costing us way more to keep carrying it with us from place to place than it would cost us to just let it go. And if we don't ever open it up and let go of some of the stuff, we are eventually going to be flying along with all that extra weight until we come crashing down in one way or another.

MORE THAN JUST A HONEYMOON SUITCASE

Because I already had my daughter Morgan when I met him, Scott got an instant family when he married me. Little did he know that along with this instant family came a whole a lot of my baggage. Since he had several serious long-term girlfriends prior to dating me, he also had his own baggage. There we were with my baggage and his baggage and carrying much more than a small honeymoon suitcase. I don't think we had any idea just exactly how much baggage we were bringing to the marriage and what we had just carried on to the longest flight we would ever take.

In addition to never dealing with the baggage that we both came with, we made a decision that ended up creating additional issues that we never saw coming. We had decided to go ahead and have a baby after our first year of marriage. I was in my last year of college and Morgan was already six years old; so, we figured that sooner rather than later was as good a time as any.

Our daughter Anna was born just a few weeks after I graduated with my bachelor's degree and, unbeknownst to us prior to her birth, she had a very rare chromosome disorder. That meant the first years of Anna's life would be consumed by pediatric specialists appointments, constant visits and surgeries at the children's hospital, therapies of every kind, five different daily prescription drugs, and medical bills upon medical bills. Add to that the medical conditions that came with having a disabled child, the daily struggles of handling her care, and still raising other children in the house. It basically piled more stress on top of everything else that had never been dealt with.

Emotional baggage doesn't discriminate, either. It doesn't matter if it comes packed up in Louie Vuitton or Samsonite. It doesn't matter if we are rich or poor, black or white, educated or blue-collar, male or female, attractive or plain, funny or serious, popular or a loner, Christian or non-religious. Underneath whatever package it is wrapped in, we all bleed the same red blood and cry the same clear salty tears. Our pain still hurts all of us uniquely and differently, yet equally and alike. No one is exempt from carrying emotional baggage of some sort. Some may be worse than others, but it all hurts and all of it will affect us even if we try to ignore it.

THE CHURCH LADY FAÇADE

As a result of all my stress and baggage, I did what any "good Christian woman" would do and I buried myself deep into church activities, volunteering for everything, and getting involved in every possible way. We had two more babies, Sarah and Clay, within five years from Anna's birth, and I stayed super busy with anything and everything that I could do at church and with the kids.

I never dealt with the disappointment of graduating college only to put my degree on a shelf and never use it in the professional world. I made that sacrifice to give Anna the best care as possible, which was very necessary. However, I never grieved the loss of my own hopes and dreams for my future. I never grieved the loss of my career as a Public Relations writer. I never dealt with the trauma of having a disabled daughter. I never grieved the loss of the dreams that I had for her life, either. I was forced to go straight into fight or flight mode and stay there for a very long time. Instead, I chose distraction over dealing with the issues and kept myself busy the best way I thought I should.

This distraction worked for a while, but eventually the baggage started to burst open. The zippers would no longer hold everything inside because it became overstuffed. At that point, I attempted to begin the process of cleaning out some of that baggage. I tiptoed around several points of pain from my past that needed to be healed, but I was careful to never dig too deep. I convinced myself that I needed to focus on my children during that season and that deep spiritual work could wait. I was careful to never open that baggage too wide or for too long.

It's amazing how we can open the suitcase just enough to remove a few things, being careful that it will zip again, but never dig any deeper to really clear it out. Sure, it will lighten the load a tad bit, but it will hardly make a difference after you've continued lugging it around with you for as long as I did. For a while, I just sat on the baggage, trying to stuff everything back in and zip it back up. I tried upgrading the outward appearance, too. Maybe a designer bag would change things, right? I wish it were that easy.

I told myself so many lies: "Just look the part, Melanie, and it will all be okay. Just keep up that façade of the perfect plastic family, and this will soon pass. You look great on the outside. No one needs to see how everything is just stuffed in there on the inside. Wear a big smile on your face and keep your hair fixed perfectly. Buy a new cute outfit. Buy matching outfits for the whole family. Tell everyone how wonderful your life is and how great your marriage is. Fake it 'til you make it. Share another 'fakebook' post about your perfect and happy family. Just lie about it until you believe the lies. Don't open that suitcase of baggage."

I was such a hypocrite. And I was miserable. Everything inside of me just wanted to burst. I knew I couldn't keep it held together forever.

I've learned that being a hypocrite will only get us so far. Sure, we can convince everyone around us that we have such a great life. But we just hurt ourselves when we do that. The picture-perfect image does nothing for our pain. We can't "fake it 'til we make it" and actually expect it to improve.

I honestly believe that faking it makes it hurt worse- *way* worse. First, there's the pain from deep within gnawing at your heart. It doesn't go away. It's a silent cry that rips you to pieces. Then, there's the isolating pain of not being able to be truthful with anyone about how much you're hurting inside. And it's not because it's not possible to be truthful. It's because you believe that it's not safe, or that no one will understand, or any number of other lies that you believe. But eventually, all baggage will burst in some way. It's inevitable.

Can you think of ways you have created your own façade? Take a moment to peak into your suitcase of baggage and examine the contents. Identify the places where you may be trying to 'fake it 'til you make it.' Do you see places of hypocrisy in your life? Are you willing to admit them to a safe person? Learn from my mistake here and don't keep that suitcase closed any longer.

Since I never really opened my suitcase and took a good hard look at the contents, my baggage eventually burst open into the biggest mess I had ever found myself in! It was a mess that couldn't be hidden with fancy labels or designer bags. It was a mess that didn't just explode in the room where it was located. Instead, it was like an explosion of epic proportions. It took the form of one of the biggest compromising and immoral decisions anyone can ever make.

REFLECTION QUESTIONS:

- What baggage are you carrying, unwilling to open it and clean it out?
- Have you created a façade to cover up the truth of your reality?

CHAPTER 4

✠ ✠ ✠

THE PERFECT FALL TO TEMPTATION

Hollywood may glamorize it. Television shows and soap operas may normalize it. Books and movies may romanticize it. But the repercussions of pain and suffering from an adulterous affair seem to go unspoken by those industries that entice us with such fantasies.

I tried to justify my choices by the fact that it seemed like everyone else was doing it and that it was the popular thing to do to 'fix' a bad marriage. Just go get my needs met elsewhere, stay married, and everyone is happy. My spouse and I won't have to go through a bitter divorce. The kids won't have to witness the destruction of our family and everything they've ever known. And I won't have to continue living without my needs for love, intimacy and significance met by my spouse.

Too bad it wasn't that simple. Too bad that Hollywood, television, books and movies lie. Too bad there's no legitimate justification for such a sin. The 'in' thing just happens to be the acceptable sin of the moment; but it doesn't change the fact that it is still sin with major repercussions. It will still damage you down to your soul and leave you hurting worse than you were before you did it.

I really believed that I could fill the gigantic hole in my heart and soul that had been caused by my marital struggles by entering a relationship with another man. I believed that I had tried everything else to solve the problem.

Though it was my first and only act of adultery, it wasn't my first attempt to fill the void with other things that the world tells us will work. It wasn't my second or third attempt, either. In fact, I had read many Christian marriage books and had attended many Christian marriage classes to heal the pain, but it was still present. I got busy in all sorts of church activities and volunteer opportunities, but it was still there. I thought that I could immerse myself in church life to somehow 'full-proof' my marriage from this growing hole in my heart. But nothing seemed to work.

Sadly, the books about how to affair-proof my marriage just made the idea of it sound even more appealing to me. Nothing seemed to work because everything I tried was a surface-level solution to a heart-level problem. Deep down, my heart just longed for my needs to be met. I was starving for something that just wasn't there in our relationship.

> *Nothing seemed to work because everything I tried was a surface-level solution to a heart-level problem.*

The longing in my heart just increased as the years passed until I was so hungry for it that I couldn't starve myself any longer. And the enemy of my soul knew exactly how to show up in the perfect package of temptation that would appear to be the exact thing my heart was craving.

That's the thing about our enemy, Satan- he is a master of disguise. He's the liar of all liars, and he's good at his job. The Bible tells us that he has one purpose in our lives: to steal, kill, and destroy (John 10:10 NKJV). But he's cunning enough to know better than just show up as a little red devil with horns and a pitchfork. He's more seductive than we think. He studies us long before he attacks. He becomes familiar with our weak points and strikes where we are most vulnerable.

Satan listens when we pray so that he knows exactly what we ask God to give us. Then, he shows up in a counterfeit version of God's best for us. It looks so much like the real thing that we can easily overlook that slight percentage of a point that it's off. This is because he comes when we are so hungry in our souls that we will take a bite of just about anything to satisfy the hunger.

The enemy of my soul knew exactly how to show up in the perfect package of temptation that would appear to be the exact thing my heart was craving.

Revelation 13:18 NKJV tells us that his number is 666. I once thought about this idea that we could just look at that number as 6.66. Did you catch the added decimal point? The added decimal point shows a number that is so very close to the whole number 7, but not quite. God's number is 7. Seven is the number of completion in the Bible. Seven is used by God many times throughout scripture. So, Satan, the great deceiver, tries to be like God and get as close to looking like a 7 as he can. But he will always fall slightly short of a 7 because he can never be for us what only God can.

If you identify any 'almost-sevens' in your life right now, I urge you to turn away! Trust me on this. What I'm about to share in the next section is still so unbelievable to me today.

THE ENEMY IN DISGUISE

It surprised me how easily I was able to make the choice to do it. All it took was the right person at the right time to notice me and give me the attention that I wasn't getting from my husband. To meet someone who made me feel significant and valued- the two most painfully triggering needs that were causes of pain in my marriage. I see now how those areas of weakness were the perfect targets to strike my already vulnerable heart. The baggage had burst, and I couldn't even begin to close it back up.

From there, the idea was planted like a small seed in my head. After that, it grew into a thought that I fantasized about for months. It was like a drug that I could use to escape from the reality of my circumstances. Eventually, it was easy to drop hints about my thoughts to this other person in a way that confirmed them. By the time we actually acted upon our thoughts, it scared me at just how easy it was for me to do something so blatantly wrong with no hesitation whatsoever. And I became like an addict, eagerly waiting for my next 'fix' and both of us lying to everyone around us about our actions. And we both became completely chained in adulterous bondage.

That's how Satan worked. He found a foothold into the door of my soul at the very weakest point and dropped an idea like a little seed. He was subtle and sly about, too. He didn't show up on the scene as something disgusting or vile that I would recognize as wrong, right away. No, he showed up disguised as exactly what I thought I was missing and needing most in my life. Even though it was a counterfeit, it was a pretty package- pretty on the outside, wrapped up perfectly, but nothing but pain and misery under all that packaging. Sadly, by the time I had untied all the ribbons and bows and unwrapped the packaging, I was far too committed to it to just put it down and walk away.

Sin is tricky like that. I'd be lying if I said that sin didn't feel good when you're in the thick of it. It's such a deception. It's like a piece of candy that starts out tasting so wonderful, like the best thing you've ever tasted in your life. You want more and more of it, and you just can't seem to get enough. It's satisfying, but only for a short while. It quickly dissolves in your mouth and disappears altogether.

You quickly find yourself needing more of it and needing it more often to meet its addictive demands. Before you know it, it's all you can think about, which makes it idolatry. And now, it's not only that one type of sin, anymore. You find yourself lying to cover it up. It's gluttony because you constantly want to consume it. You've lost all self-control. There's no peace in your life because you're constantly sneaking around and having to watch your back. But it feels good in the moment that you ask yourself, "how do I ever stop?"

All the while, your spirit feels like it's slowly dying. Because it IS dying! You're now so fat from too much of this sin-candy and you feel miserable. Life is full of extreme highs and extreme lows. In the moment, it feels great. But all the rest of the time you either spend fantasizing about the next time or spend feeling the extreme shame and guilt that always accompanies such sin.

THERE'S NO CONDEMNATION IN CHRIST

As I said before, committing adultery was definitely NOT something that I just casually decided to do one day. It's not what I dreamed about when I was thinking about my future. I know I never would have wanted to have that added to my already full baggage. I had a strong conviction about right and wrong. I *knew* better. I can't even pretend that I was naïve about my actions. I may have been deceived by the enemy's ploys, but I wasn't oblivious about the compromise I was making. I knew full well that I was going against everything I had ever been taught and believed. That's the worst part of it. I can't blame it on ignorance or not knowing full well that I was *deliberately choosing* sin.

In the beginning of this book, I told you how I liked to play pretend with my Barbie dolls. I was like most kids my age who played with all the popular toys of the time. I watched Saturday morning cartoons every weekend and Wonder Woman on primetime. I would jump off things everywhere I went like I was a superhero, too. And even though my life had some major dysfunction that happened behind closed doors, I was able to experience a mostly normal kid-of-the-80's childhood.

In addition to my Barbie dolls, I also had several G.I. Joe dolls that I played with when the neighbor boy would come over. We played war games, played at the nearby creek, and constantly came home with ticks in our hair from the woods by our house. I suppose there was a little tomboy in me, as well.

I loved to climb trees and sing songs with my microphone in front of the mirror in my bedroom. I actually wanted to be a singer like my favorite singer Amy Grant, or be part of my favorite group the Go-Go's, when I grew up; so I constantly practiced in my room. We had a clubhouse on stilts in our backyard that my brother accidentally burned down to the ground, one summer. We had a metal swing set that constantly flipped over if we swung too high, and there was a trampoline in the neighbor's backyard that we jumped to from his roof. We had an endless number of ways to use our imagination if we ever claimed that we were bored.

It's accurate to say that boredom rarely got me into trouble as a kid because I stayed busy with fun indoor and outdoor activities. Looking back, I wish I could say that I *never* got into trouble because my childhood activities kept me so occupied. Unfortunately, there was still an occasional open door for trouble.

As I fast-forward to the point in my story when adultery entered my mind, and eventually became my decision to act upon, I can also attribute some boredom to my downfall. Becoming so uninvolved in all of my previous activities had left me with too much unstructured time and very little, if not zero, accountability. Plus, there were so many more open doors for trouble.

It's layers upon layers of circumstances that cause a person to become so susceptible to making that kind of choice. It has taken me many years to be able to put some of them into words for this book. I don't think that I would have ever shared this part of my story in a book for just anyone to read and know about me if it hadn't been for God's voice telling my spirit to write it. He prompted me to share it because it's a sin with which many other people are struggling. And it was the same voice of God that had spoke to my spirit to NOT open that screen door as a kid. Most assuredly, I've learned to listen to that voice!

Just as I typed that last sentence, I thought to myself, "Too bad you didn't listen to God's voice telling your spirit NOT to commit adultery in the first place!" Yes, I acknowledge I missed an important "don't open that door" moment. And yes, now I'm writing a book about a subject that no one wants to write about, especially as the guilty party. That voice of condemnation would love to silence me and keep this story from ever reaching print.

Maybe that same voice is condemning you on the other side of this page. Please trust that God is such a redeemer Who is using this mess that I created to heal me and help you at the same time! He is not the voice of condemnation that you and I are hearing. He is the voice of forgiveness telling us that we are already forgiven if we will just admit that we are wrong, accept His forgiveness, and turn away from our sin. How could anyone not love an awesome God like that?

"There is therefore now no condemnation to those who are in Christ Jesus, who do not walk according to the flesh, but according to the Spirit."
Romans 8:1 NKJV

THE GIFT OF FREE WILL

Did you pick up this book because its title spoke to you? Have you ever read a book on this topic before? Maybe you're not sure about it because it's got all of this 'God talk' in it; or it's hitting a little too close to home and you feel a bit exposed. I say to you- please don't put it down yet! Hang with me for a while longer. I've been where you are!

I understand what it's like to believe that God can't possibly be all good and for our best interest all the time. I understand what it's like to read a book and just skim past all the scriptures because they just don't seem to resonate. I understand being in an environment where the people around me don't discuss the Bible at all, much less discuss how it has helped with a specific problem in their lives. It can feel uncomfortable at first. It can feel downright foreign. But trust me- God's Word heals us like nothing else! My love for His Word didn't just appear overnight. It has developed over years of studying scripture and letting it change the way I think about everything.

I can go one step further and say that I even understand what it's like to go through a season of questioning the very existence of God. I didn't just hear His voice speak to my spirit that one time when I was 6 years old and become completely obedient to Him for the rest of my life, never ever questioning His presence from that day forward. I wish! No, I made plenty of other mistakes along the way. And I turned my back on Him a lot. I got completely immersed in the ways of the world and found success there. I enjoyed all the charm that a world away from God offers a person. I chose disobedience and my way of doing things too many times to count.

I also understand having been taught the wrong belief that God can be mean and judgmental and will just send us to Hell for any little mess-up or sin. Don't get me wrong, He IS a holy and just God. He is serious about us turning away from sin. His judgement is real. But *our* choices determine the outcome. He isn't *sending* us to Hell. Our deliberate and willful wrong choices put us on the broad road leading in that direction. We must own that fact. He is actually so gracious to just keep offering us exit ramps from our road of sin. The narrow road is one exit ramp away!

He gives every single one of us endless chances to repent and turn back to Him to save us, as long as we have breath in our lungs.

We *will* run out of chances though. When our last day on this planet comes without warning, there will be no more exit ramps. The road that we are on will have led us to our destination. We make the choice as to where we will end up. If we don't like where we are currently headed, we must listen to Him and do what He tells us.

> *If we don't like where we are currently headed, we must listen to Him and do what He tells us.*

Matthew chapter 7 speaks to this truth perfectly:

> *Enter through the narrow gate. For wide is the gate and broad is the road that leads to destruction, and many enter through it. But small is the gate and narrow is the road that leads to life, and only a few find it.*
> *Matthew 7:13-14 NIV*

Like I said before, it would have been so much easier and saved me a lot of grief to have just made the decision to never question His voice from that day forward- to listen to those 'don't open that door' moments. But I believe that one of the reasons He allows us to have free will- to think and do as we want- is so that we will gain an appreciation for His wisdom through the lessons we learn from our wrong choices. And hopefully, we will also start to use our free will to make better choices and choose Him.

Of course, He gave us free will so that loving Him would be our choice, not forced upon us. That's the main reason. But free will also allows us the freedom to choose sin or to *not* choose sin. Both choices come with consequences- good or bad. It's our choice.

Free will has been given to mankind since the beginning of time, starting with Adam and Eve. Yet, God put parameters in place right from the start because He loved us. He gave the first people of creation the beautiful Garden of Eden to live in perfect relationship with Him. Adam and Eve had everything they needed. They lived in total freedom. They lived in perfection. They had authority over everything that God had given them. Their lives were not tainted with sin or evil of any kind. God wanted to keep them safe and secure from those evils. So, He gave them complete freedom and only one rule for their protection: do not eat from this one tree- the tree of the knowledge of good and evil.

> *"Then the Lord God took the man and put him in the garden of Eden to tend and keep it. And the Lord God commanded the man, saying, "Of every tree of the garden you may freely eat; but of the tree of the knowledge of good and evil you shall not eat, for in the day that you eat of it you shall surely die.""*
>
> *Genesis 2:15-17 NKJV*

Be sure to take note the very important fact from this passage above: They were free to eat from *every single tree* of the garden, except *one*. That's a very minimal restriction if you ask me. In our current world that is consumed with rules and regulations that must be followed every day, it's hard to wrap my brain around what it would have been like to live with *just one single rule*. Yet, that's all Adam and Eve had to follow. Add to that the wonderful gift of free will and we get a glimpse of freedom that no human has ever experienced since Eden. Free to choose anything they wanted, even free to choose to obey or disobey the one rule they had been given- a rule that was put in place so they wouldn't *die*.

So why would it be so hard to follow one single simple rule that would save them from death? I suppose we could ask ourselves the same question. Why do we have such a hard time obeying God for *our* own good? We focus on what we *can't* have instead of all that we DO have. And that's where Satan plays his best game of deceit. If he can keep our focus stuck on our discontentment long enough, he can convince us that our sin is okay. He will even get us to question what God *really* said in the first place.

> *"Now the serpent was more cunning than any beast of the field which the Lord God had made. And he said to the woman, "Has God indeed said, 'You shall not eat of every tree of the garden'?"*
>
> *And the woman said to the serpent, "We may eat the fruit of the trees of the garden; but of the fruit of the tree*

which is in the midst of the garden, God has said, 'You shall not eat it, nor shall you touch it, lest you die.' "

Then the serpent said to the woman, "You will not surely die. For God knows that in the day you eat of it your eyes will be opened, and you will be like God, knowing good and evil."

So when the woman saw that the tree was good for food, that it was pleasant to the eyes, and a tree desirable to make one wise, she took of its fruit and ate. She also gave to her husband with her, and he ate.

Then the eyes of both of them were opened, and they knew that they were naked; and they sewed fig leaves together and made themselves coverings.

And they heard the sound of the Lord God walking in the garden in the cool of the day, and Adam and his wife hid themselves from the presence of the Lord God among the trees of the garden.

Then the Lord God called to Adam and said to him, "Where are you?"

So he said, "I heard Your voice in the garden, and I was afraid because I was naked; and I hid myself."

And He said, "Who told you that you were naked? Have you eaten from the tree of which I commanded you that you should not eat?"

Then the man said, "The woman whom You gave to be with me, she gave me of the tree, and I ate."

And the Lord God said to the woman, "What is this you have done?"

The woman said, "The serpent deceived me, and I ate.""
Genesis 3:1, 3-13 NKJV

There are so many lessons to be learned from this passage of scripture. I could probably write a whole other book about it. But I'm just going to pull a list of take-away points from it:

> ➢ Point 1: The serpent twisted God's words right from the start. God had said that Adam and Eve could eat from every tree except one. The serpent asked if God had really said that they should not eat from every tree. And he left off the part about it being just one tree. Just a slight manipulation of

words, enough to create doubt in her understanding of what God really said, and to make God's one rule seem more restrictive than it really was.

➢ Point 2: The serpent made her question God's words and motive. When Eve restated God's rule with the correct wording, the serpent used his next tactic. He dismissed the consequence of death for breaking the one rule and he made her question God's motive for making the rule. "You will not surely die... you will be like God." Modern-day version of this: "Nothing bad will really happen. God just doesn't want you to be true to yourself. He knows that if you eat it, you'll be like Him."

➢ Point 3: The serpent tempted her desire to be like God and planted a seed of pride that she could be her own god, knowing good and evil. Pride says that we don't need a god to tell us what's best for us, that we can navigate this life just fine without him.

➢ Point 4: The serpent appealed to her desires for something that tasted good and promised wisdom. Neither one of those desires are bad when they are fulfilled God's way.

Since I'm a southern girl, I'll give you a good southern example of fulfilling a desire in an unhealthy way. Here it goes: God created cows for us to eat their meat- the beef. Beef is a healthy source of protein for our bodies (sorry to all the vegetarians reading this). We southerners take that beef, cut it into a patty and dip it in a starchy batter and deep fry it in greasy cooking oil and call it chicken fried steak. Then, we cover it in fatty gravy and sprinkle it with tons of salt and pepper. Not so healthy! It tastes really good, but it can lead to high cholesterol, high blood pressure and obesity. We took the desire for something good and created something not so good, something that is actually really BAD for our health. If we eat this way all the time, it will eventually kill us.

And about wisdom- it is good to desire wisdom. But we must be careful not to use our desire for wisdom to convince ourselves that we can become wiser than God.

➢ Point 5: The serpent's temptation left them with shame. As soon as they ate the fruit from the tree of the knowledge of good and evil, they covered themselves with fig leaves. They were ashamed of their nakedness. Shame- Satan's favorite chain of bondage. If he can get us to feel shame, he can cause us to hide ourselves from God. Shame is such an important topic that we will revisit it later in the book.

➢ Point 6: The serpent's temptation caused them to displace blame and become divided. When God questioned them about who had told them they were naked, Adam immediately blamed Eve and said, "the woman whom you gave to me, she gave me of the tree." Adam didn't take responsibility for his choice to eat the fruit, and his statement "the woman whom you gave me" divided himself from Eve. Then, Eve displaced blame to the serpent, also failing to take responsibility for her choice.

Adam and Eve were full of shame, hiding from God, blaming someone else, and becoming divided. Sin had entered the world and the enemy had gained ground. It's not a coincidence that Satan still uses the exact same tactics today. Since the history of humanity began in Genesis, he has found ways to shame us, separate us from God, convince us to blame others and divide us from each other. And dividing marriages is one of the highest on his list of priorities. This is warfare, people!

Satan has wanted to divide marriage since God first created it with Adam and Eve. Marriage is a picture of God's relationship with His people. We are called "the bride of Christ."

"I promised you as a pure bride to one husband- Christ."
2 Corinthians 11:2b NLT

&

"Husbands, love your wives, just as Christ also loved the church and gave Himself for her, that He might sanctify and cleanse her with the washing of water by the Word, that He might present her to Himself a glorious church, not having spot or wrinkle or any such thing, but that she should be holy and without blemish."
Ephesians 5:25-27 NKJV

Satan's divisive plans are to accomplish many goals, and ultimately one major goal. Divided marriages equal divided families. Divided families equal divided homes. Divided homes equal divided people. Divided people equal a divided nation. And a divided nation has the potential to seep in and divide the church. When he divides the church, he will attempt to divide the people completely from God.

There I found myself, feeling divided from my husband and divided from God. I had put myself in this position and had no idea how to get out. It was lonely and painful. The sin candy had dissolved and left me with much more than just a toothache. It was the worst kind of ache- a heartache- a heart that ached for relationship with my Heavenly Father again.

> *Satan's ultimate goal is to divide people completely from God.*

REFLECTION QUESTIONS:

- Where are you in your relationship with God?
- Do you feel separated and alone?
- Are you questioning everything about Him?
- Are you willing to listen to Him?
- Are you willing to do the work to allow Him to pull you out of your pit? If yes, I pray that the next section of this book will help you take those steps.

PART TWO

CLIMBING OUT OF THE PIT OF DESPAIR

CHAPTER 5

✠ ✠ ✠

COULD MY MARRIAGE BE SAVED?

Here I was, sitting in the middle of the aftermath of a giant tsunami that had burst through my home with catastrophic force, leaving a wreckage of shame, guilt, broken trust, pain, and division. My heart ached for God's presence. It seemed like the enemy had won.

> *It was my own self-inflicted painful division from my Heavenly Father who still loved me so much and wanted to be close to me again.*

Shame and guilt were heavy and burdensome chains that tied me down to the pit of despair and convinced me that I would never escape. At one point, I gave up trying to escape. I had caused so much pain to myself and the people around me that I felt all alone and abandoned by God. But the truth was that God never abandoned me. *My sin* had created division between God and me. It was my own self-inflicted painful division from my Heavenly Father who still loved me so much and wanted to be close to me again.

WHAT IS DESPAIR?

Despair was definitely my rock-bottom. Despair is defined as a complete loss of hope. Hopeless. Defeated. Destitute. At a loss.

There's no deeper bottom than rock-bottom. Mine was found at the bottom of a deep dark pit.

My deep dark pit of despair was painful and ugly. I was mourning the loss of something that felt very real to me at the time. The enemy had fooled me- hook, line, and sinker. I had fallen for his sin bait that turned out to be a fake fishing lure just dangling in the deep ocean of my problems. It seemed real until I bit it. Once I bit it, I was caught up in it so quickly that I never had time to contemplate the question of whether or not it was really real. And now, I was discarded like a diseased fish in a pile of waste. A pit of waste. A pit of despair.

I had landed in my pit of despair by my own choice. I am the one who took a bite of the bait. I am the one that was deceived into believing I could turn a gigantic sinful decision into something meaningful. I couldn't blame anyone else. No one else could truly understand the pain that I lived with every day. Nobody but Jesus. Yet, I felt so distant from Him that I didn't even try to reach out and pray.

I would just go through the motions at church, too. I raised my hands in worship, feeling no connection to God. I felt nothing at all. Except numbness. The same God that spoke to the younger me was not speaking now. Or at least, I wasn't hearing. I can't say that I was really listening, either. I was empty and void of meaning in life. I liked my pity party just a little bit. I chose to dwell in my "pit" party.

Deep down, I thought that God might just feel sorry enough for me to just go ahead and give me what I wanted. I can almost laugh about that, now. A toddler throws a fit to get what they want. My depressive state was like an adult version of a toddler fit, hoping I would still get what I wanted. That sin nature still screaming out to feed my flesh. My soul too weak to fight for anything.

I had days that I didn't want to get out of bed and face it. I can't say for sure if I suffered from depression because I still had to force myself to function. I'm thankful for my young children whose needs required me to get up and get moving every day. I'm thankful for a disabled child who needed me to care for her. I could keep moving through each day just going through the motions and staying in the pit of despair in my mind. It was a hidden pit. No one on the outside could see it. And no one on the outside could get me out of it. I was the only one who could decide if I *wanted* out and wanted to do the work to get out.

It's tempting to just decide that it's going to take too much work to clean up the mess, so we just resolve to move on from there and let it go. That might have been the easier choice. I actually thought about it for a while. I filed for a divorce. I thought that getting out of our marriage would be the best and easiest choice for everyone involved. Escape the destruction and start fresh. Never look deep within myself and deal with questions of 'why' and 'how' I ended up here in the first place. Never open the baggage. Just stay in my pit of despair and remodel it with cute new decorations. Maybe do some more surface work so I can fool everyone around me into thinking that I was working on everything. Create another fake "got it all together" version of myself. The truth was that I was already so good at it! I played the church lady façade so well that most people had no idea about the entire adulterous affair in the first place.

I didn't miss a beat when it came to playing the role of the happy, put-together Christian wife and mom who juggled all my titles so well. No one really had to know. If I could convince everyone else, then *surely,* I would believe it for myself. Smile bigger and laugh harder. Have fun! Keep volunteering to the maximum capacity. Focus on the kids and their talents. Get really fit and be a gym rat. Write funny, catchy social media posts. Write another inspiring blog entry. Oh, I knew how to pretend like it was all okay. I learned that type of coping skill a long time ago.

But reality tells me that it's not that easy to keep up that pretense forever. At some point, I would cave in. It may not be another tsunami level of destruction. But a fault line that existed on the surface of my soul certainly went deeper. And a little earthquake could still do damage. Damage is damage, no matter how small it looks on the surface.

Once again, I remind you that joy is internal. It is not affected by the external things around us. All those external 'improvements' would not solve anything. And running away from the problems wasn't the solution, either.

I didn't go through with the divorce. I let it sit for six months. For six months, I went back and forth contemplating whether I wanted to enter that mess of a battle that takes place on the battleground of divorce court. I had several questions to ask myself. Did I want to give up and call it quits? Would quitting be easier or harder? Was I willing to try to work it out if I stayed? What were my motives for staying? Could my marriage be saved??

GOD OF THE IMPOSSIBLE

That last question was actually the easiest to answer. Yes, without a doubt, my marriage could be saved. It was not impossible. God is the God of all things possible. Luke 1:37 (NKJV) says: *"For with God nothing will be impossible."* Did you catch that key word: 'nothing?' So, the question about whether my marriage *could* be saved was less about God's ability to save it and more about my desire to *want* to save it.

When Jesus paid the price for all of mankind on that old, rugged cross at Calvary, He paid it for the worst sinner you could ever think about who would ever live on planet Earth just as much as He paid it for the most innocent person you've ever known. No one is beyond the saving power of Christ. And that means that NO sin-caused devastation is beyond Christ's saving power. The worst marriage disaster ever is not too big for our God.

I was left with facing the fact that if saving my marriage was not a question about Christ's power and ability to save it, then it was a question about *my desire* to want to save it. It boiled down to what my choice would be and whether I was willing to do the work. I had opened that door to sin by my own choice, and I had to close the door by my own choice. It was another defining moment. The navigation system was in my hand. Was I going to correct the direction and change my course? Was I going to take the next on-ramp back to the narrow road? And was I going to put forth the effort to redefine my future?

Ask yourself the same questions. Are you willing to do the work to save your marriage? Are you going to correct your direction? If you are divorced, are you willing to do the work to truly heal your soul? No matter your situation, are you going to put forth the effort to redefine your future?

DID I *WANT* TO SAVE MY MARRIAGE?

I had some serious questions to ponder. Each day comprised of asking myself those questions and making a decision for THAT day. Small defining moments. I *still* have days when I must ask myself those questions. Even after all these years, there are still hard days.

Don't let that last statement discourage you. It's my own personal problem. You will soon discover that I have been one of the most stubborn people on the planet. I take twice, if not three times as long, to make the obedient choice. I'm getting better, though. Life lessons are great instructors for obedience. I get a lot of them. They are maturing me. I choose obedience over my own ways more often now than before. Finally!

I stayed still for a very long time, focusing on that most important question: did I *want* to save my marriage? Followed by: what was my motivation for staying? And was I willing to work it out if I stayed?

I felt like I was frozen in time, unable to make a decision at all. I was afraid of making the *wrong* decision. My feelings were completely out of whack and my heart was a wreck. I wanted to believe the fantasy that I kept playing over and over again in my head that it had been a *real* relationship, and that it hadn't really ended. I wanted to believe that it was just on pause while I ended my marriage so we could be together the *right* way.

The *right* way?!? What a fantasy! What a lie! There was nothing *right* about that relationship that had started in the context of sin. Sure, God is a God who redeems; but I certainly should have known better than to want to enter back into willful and deliberate sin with the hope that God would redeem it.

The apostle Paul addressed this misconception of trying to use God's endless grace as a justification for choosing willful and deliberate sin in Romans chapters 5 and 6:

> *"God's law was given so that all people could see how sinful they were. But as people sinned more and more, God's wonderful grace became more abundant. So just as sin ruled over all people and brought them to death, now God's wonderful grace rules instead, giving us right standing with God and resulting in eternal life through Jesus Christ our Lord."*
> *Romans 5: 20-21 NLT*

&

> *"Well then, should we keep on sinning so that God can show us more and more of his wonderful grace? Of course not! Since we have died to sin, how can we continue to live in it?"*
> *Romans 6: 1-2 NLT*

&

"If we deliberately keep on sinning after we have received the knowledge of the truth, no sacrifice for sins is left, but only fearful expectation of judgement and of raging fire that will consume the enemies of God."
Hebrews 10: 26-27 NIV

Choosing ongoing willful deliberate sin was NOT the answer. I was supposed to be *dying* to sin, not deliberately choosing it. Listening to my feelings and following my heart was NOT the answer. Living in a fantasy world was DEFINITELY NOT the answer. And staying stuck in a state of perpetual pit dwelling was the absolute worst thing I could decide to do if I ever wanted to improve the situation.

> *Choosing ongoing willful deliberate sin was NOT the answer.*

I want to stop right here for a minute and park on that statement. What exactly do I mean by 'improve the situation?' First of all, I'll tell you what I *don't* mean. I don't mean improving anything on the external level at all. All of those 'improvements' that I described earlier would not fix this. I'm going to dig into this idea much more in chapter 6. But for now, I just want to touch on it for a little bit to make sure you follow where I'm going with it.

The improvement had to start *inside* of me. Long before anything changed on the outside, I had to get intensely honest about what was happening *within*. If I wanted to honestly answer the question about wanting to save my marriage, then I had to be willing to take an honest look at the condition of my heart.

> *Long before anything changed on the outside, I had to get intensely honest about what was happening within.*

TAKING A GOOD HARD LOOK AT MY HEART

When I refer to my heart, I'm talking about my soul. Our souls are comprised of our mind, will and emotions. It's where we store all our memories and everything uniquely about us. It's the driving force to how we filter life experiences and make decisions. By 'filter,' I mean the way we process life.

If we were raised in a spiritually and emotionally healthy environment, we have a better chance of having a healthy filter. If we grew up with dysfunction in our home, the filter can be more smudged than others. No matter the circumstance, all of life's experiences affect our filter in some way.

A mean teacher in school. A playground bully who targeted us. An insecurity about our physical appearance. A learning disability. Lack of athletic abilities. Lack of talent in the arts. A friend who betrayed us. A friend who rejected us. A social group that excluded us. A coach who manipulated us. A boyfriend or girlfriend who dumped us. A teen pregnancy. An abortion. A miscarriage. A controlling partner. An abusive partner. A divorce. A church hurt. A job that stressed us out. A boss who ridiculed us. A wayward sibling or child. A parent who died young. A child who died unexpectedly. Abuse. Addiction. Unmet expectations. These are only a handful of experiences that create smudges on our filters. You get the idea.

A smudge on our filter affects the way we view an experience and the way we react to an experience. Without even realizing that I was doing it, I was reacting to Scott's actions through the smudged lenses of my filter.

If I had written this chapter in this book six months ago, I wouldn't have been able to put words to describe a few of the smudges on my filter. They were still buried deep beneath the surface. I am only recently aware of them. These two big triggers for reaction from me that I mentioned earlier in the book were insignificance and disregard. Some other triggers were emotional abandonment, rejection, trauma, and judgment.

When I say 'trigger,' I am referring to an uncharacteristic past-person response to a present-day cause. It's when our present-day self reacts in a way that is uncharacteristic for us, so clearly being caused by an underlying unhealed hurt or trauma from the past. It's when a past version of ourselves, many times from childhood, surfaces in an instant because a present situation took us right back to something that was never validated and healed the first time around in the past. And until we recognize it for what it is, name it and deal with it, it will continue to trigger us.

Insignificance and disregard stemmed back to childhood wounds for me. And while I wasn't aware of them until just recently, they had been there all along. They were buried deep beneath other layers of pain that had to be healed first.

I will give you a quick example of a trigger to which most of us can relate. When Scott chose to work late and not call home to tell me he was working late at the office, my smudged filter said that I was insignificant to Scott and not valued enough to be priority-that I was not worth the time to make a phone call. If I tried calling him to make sure he was okay and he didn't answer, my belief of insignificance and his disregard for my concerns cut even deeper.

Yes, it would have been respectful and responsible of him to come home on time if he could, or at least call home if he couldn't. That is his part to own in the problem. But my part to own is my complete overreaction to a very common marriage issue.

My subconscious beliefs of being insignificant and disregarded were being triggered by Scott; and they contributed to a problem that was much deeper than either of us were aware. I'm not making light of the fact that Scott carried faults of his own in our marriage problems. I'm just owning the fact that I was processing them through broken filters that made them *look* and *feel* much worse than they may have actually been. And this book is meant to take ownership for *our* parts in our situations.

Despite the issues that Scott may have contributed to our marriage, my heart issues were major contributors to the problem.

"The heart is deceitful above all things, and desperately wicked; who can know it?"
Jeremiah 17:9 NKJV

Not only did I have unhealed hurts deep in my soul that I had yet to discover, but I had an *adulterous heart*. I believe that an adulterous heart is best defined as having a spirit that says, "I love God and want to live according to His Will;" but being continually lured away by the temptations of the world.

An adulterous heart is never willing to give up *all* its own ways. There's always that *one thing* that we try to carry with us into our new redeemed life, but it just won't work.

Here's an example of how my adulterous heart operated. Every time I didn't like the way something was going, I wanted to bail out. In my mind, I would argue with God about whatever the issue was that I was struggling with. If I didn't like His answer or His way, I would decide that I knew what was best for me and didn't need His intervention anyways. And this way of thinking hadn't started in my marriage. It didn't start in adolescence, either. It had started way back as a child.

> *An adulterous heart is never willing to give up all its own ways. There's always that one thing that we try to carry with us into our new redeemed life, but it just won't work.*

AN ADULTEROUS HEART

We've all been in the supermarket when someone's child is throwing a screaming tantrum. Honestly, I bet most of us could say that one of our own kids has done this at least once. And I bet if we think back long and hard to when we were very young, most of us can recall our *own* supermarket fits. I know I can!

Being the oldest of four kids, I was the ringleader of my mom's stressful supermarket trips. We got so bad at wreaking havoc in the supermarket that she finally just started leaving us in the car while she filled and purchased an entire cart of groceries for our ungrateful selves. I wouldn't recommend leaving your kids in the car in today's time, but we were mostly safe back then.

It was the 80's. I lived in a small town with a population less than 15,000. And the Piggly Wiggly grocery store had windows all the way across the front of the store. Mom could easily see us every time she rounded the corner to the next aisle at the front of the store. Plus, who in their right mind would steal a car full of bratty kids hanging out the windows and climbing all over the top, yelling at every person that passed by? I sure wouldn't!

While the supermarket fit throwing had landed my siblings and I in the parking lot while my mom shopped, I guess I didn't quite learn my lesson about the consequences of throwing fits. I just changed my fit-throwing style.

Adult fit throwing basically goes like this: If God doesn't give me my way, I'll just do what I want, anyway. I don't need God to tell me what to do all the time, especially if He isn't going to answer my demanding prayers how I think they should be answered. His way is no fun and goes against who I am. I'm a person who goes for what I want. Isn't God the One who made me this way in the first place? And He should want me to be happy. Maybe if I pretend like I don't know I'm sinning, He will give me a pass and let me keep this sin that I like so much. I'll play the ignorant card and act like I didn't hear Him in the first place. I'll just surround myself with people who tell me what I want to hear. I'll gather a group of supporters for my sin. I'll just put other things at a higher priority than my relationship with Him. A lower accountability means less rules anyways, right? I want what I want, and I'll try whatever method that might get it for me. Surely, God will give in to me eventually.

Anyone relate to this type of adult fit throwing? I know I'm not alone. If I was alone in having ever thought like this, then there would be a lot less stories in the Bible about people like this who also had an adulterous heart. The people of the Bible were constantly unfaithful to God. They built false idols to worship instead of worshiping the one true living God. They were constantly being lured away from a right relationship with Him by the idols of this life. The world's pleasures constantly seduced them into sinful choices. They claimed to love God but were easily captivated by the temptations this world constantly throws at us. God's discipline and wrath was poured out on them many times.

"They will recognize how hurt I am by their unfaithful hearts and lustful eyes that long for their idols. Then at last they will hate themselves for all their detestable sins."
Ezekiel 6:9 NLT

People haven't really changed since Bible times. Sure, we have traded sack cloths for a t-shirt and jeans, and sandals for tennis shoes; but interestingly enough, we still sin the same way as mankind has sinned since the beginning of time. We've just gotten more creative in relabeling our sins with a title of justification. We mask gossip as a 'concerned prayer request' and greed and materialism as 'the American Dream' and all the various forms of sexual sin as 'friends with benefits', 'test drive before you buy', and 'love is love.' We get as many followers and supporters as we can, and we change the culture to fit our agendas. We make all our ways of doing things the 'new norm' and call the Bible outdated and old-fashioned. We call the people who live according to the Bible "judgmental" or "bigots." We turn the narrative completely around and call anyone who doesn't support us "hateful." But all our tactics are really just a very sneaky form of adult fit throwing. God is not fooled, and we won't outsmart His ways. He loves us too much to satisfy our sinful natures.

For a while, I tried to justify the adultery. I tried to gather supporters around me, too. Even though most people in society, whether a Christian or not, would agree that adultery is a sin, it's a bit appalling to admit that I found quite a few who were excited to hear every single detail of my 'exciting life.' After all, Hollywood has made many millions of dollars by glamorizing this very sin on the big screen! I don't have to name all the titles of movies about sexual sin that were box office hits to drive home this point. We all can name a few, I'm sure.

Well, God's not interested in what Hollywood thinks or what people flock to the theatres to watch on opening night. And, He certainly wasn't swayed by my growing number of supporters, either. Sin is sin. God's ways stay the same yesterday, today and tomorrow.

This may sound harsh to some people, but I can't shy away from sharing the truth. God loves you too much to leave you trapped in deception. Each one of us will stand before our righteous and Holy God and give an account for our lives. We will stand before Him *alone*. It won't matter how many people we got to support our sinful choices in this life when we stand before Him. We won't be judged by what the world said was acceptable, either. Our lives will be measured by God's Word alone. I won't do you any favors by trying to sugarcoat this Truth. I am a sinner in need of the saving grace of

Jesus, every day; and I have a responsibility to share what God has spoken to me through His Word. In James 4:4-8 NLT, we are warned about friendship with the world.

"You adulterers! Don't you realize that friendship with the world makes you an enemy of God? I say it again: If you want to be a friend of the world, you make yourself an enemy of God. Do you think the Scriptures have no meaning? They say that God is passionate that the spirit he has placed within us should be faithful to him. And he gives grace generously. As the Scriptures say, "God opposes the proud but gives grace to the humble."

So humble yourselves before God. Resist the devil, and he will flee from you. Come close to the God, and God will come close to you. Wash your hands, you sinner; purify your hearts, for your loyalty is divided between God and the world."
James 4: 4-8 NLT

Although I got a lot of people to support my sin, I'm thankful for a dear friend of mine who spoke the truth in love to me when I needed to hear it most. She was willing to go against the grain and stand firm in God's Word on the subject. She stood for Truth, and Truth finally got through to me. Friend, I want to be that person for YOU! If you are headed off a cliff, I'm going to warn you!

When I was finally willing to admit the truth that my choice was a sin, and I decided to take an honest look at my rebellion, I slowly started to believe that my marriage could be saved. The Truth had never changed. I knew it all along. It was just *head* knowledge that needed to become *heart* knowledge.

My sin had separated me from God. He still loved me, but I had strayed far away from Him. The growing distance from Him caused me to lose sight of His Word. The first step to moving closer to Him was to acknowledge my sin for the truth of what it was and to repent from it.

Each step away from sin and toward God was a step in the direction of healing. A step towards Truth. It felt like baby steps all over again. I had to start with the elementary truths of God's grace and build from there. Little by little, the truth replaced the lies and I felt myself growing closer to Him again.

Dear friend, today is the day for you to start taking the same steps! Kick pride to the curb and get honest with yourself about your rebellious choices. See them for what they really are: sin. Next, meditate on the truth that God loves you so much that He doesn't want to leave you this way. He sent Jesus to save you. You are not too far gone! And your sin does not have to identify you!

"Quit dabbling in sin. Purify your inner life. Quit playing the field. Hit bottom, and cry your eyes out. The fun and games are over. Get serious, really serious. Get down on your knees before the Master; it's the only way you'll get on your feet."
James 4: 9-10 MSG

CHRIST DIED FOR ALL SINS

I said it earlier in the chapter and I'm going to say it again. Christ died for ALL sins. The worst sinner on the planet is not too far from God's grace. This may be hard for some people to accept because there are people in this world who have done some horrific things. But that's the beauty of God's grace. He doesn't exclude anyone who is willing to ask for forgiveness. God sent Jesus to die to save ALL of us. His love goes beyond the worst sin. Our response is to accept His grace and forgiveness and turn away from our sin.

"But God demonstrates His own love for us in this: While we were still sinners, Christ died for us."
Romans 5:8 NIV

&

"For I am convinced that neither death nor life, neither angels nor demons, neither present nor future, nor any powers, neither height nor depth, nor anything else in all creation, will be able to separate us from the love of God that is in Christ Jesus our Lord."
Romans 8: 38-39 NIV

> *Nothing can separate us from the love of God, but sin separates us from our relationship with God.*

Nothing can separate us from the *love* of God, but sin separates us from our *relationship* with God. God loves us no matter what. But *we* have a responsibility to repent from our sins. 'Repent' in the Bible means to change your mind and to turn away. Changing our mind about our sin is to accept the spiritual conviction that we feel in our spirit and acknowledge that our sin is wrong. Once we acknowledge the conviction, we turn *away* from that sin, which turns us *towards* God.

If we don't turn away, our sin will continue to hurt us and ruin our lives. When we *choose* to continue in sin, we turn *away* from *God*, which is the exact opposite of repenting. We sabotage the relationship *by our own actions*. We are the ones causing distance and division in the relationship.

> *"It's your sins that have cut you off from God. Because of your sins, he has turned away and will not listen anymore."*
> *Isaiah 59: 2 NLT*

King David from the book of 2 Samuel understood how important the act of repentance was to return to a right relationship with God. David had committed adultery with Bathsheba, the wife of a man named Urriah. Then, Bathsheba informed David that she was pregnant with his child. David's way of covering up the scandalous pregnancy was to ultimately have Urriah killed in the front lines of battle and to bring Bathsheba into the palace as his own wife. God sent the prophet Nathan to deliver a message to David, telling him that the child conceived in adultery would die because of his sins. You can read this story in 2 Samuel 11-12 NLT.

After the death of his infant son, David lamented, and this can be found in Psalm 51. I would like to share part of it with you here:

> *"Have mercy on me, O God, because of your unfailing love. Because of your great compassion, blot out the stain*

of my sins. Wash me clean from my guilt. Purify me from my sin. For I recognize my rebellion; it haunts me day and night. Against you, and you alone, have I sinned; I have done what is evil in your sight. You will be proved right in what you say, and your judgment against me is just. For I was a sinner- yes, from the moment my mother conceived me. But you desire honesty from the womb, teaching me wisdom even there.

Purify me from my sins, and I will be clean; wash me, and I will be whiter than snow. Oh, give me back my joy again; you have broken me- now let me rejoice. Don't keep looking at my sins. Remove the stain of my guilt. Create in me a clean heart, O God. Renew a loyal spirit within me. DO not banish me from your presence, and don't take your Holy Spirit from me.

Restore to me the joy of your salvation, and make me willing to obey you. Then I will teach your ways to rebels, and they will return to you. Forgive me for shedding blood, O God who saves; then I will joyfully sing of your forgiveness. Unseal my lips, O Lord, that my mouth may praise you.You do not desire a sacrifice or I would offer one. You do not want a burnt offering. The sacrifice you desire is a broken spirit. You will not reject a broken and repentant heart, O God."
Psalm 51:1-17 NLT

Here is a well-known person in scripture who committed both adultery AND murder. Yet, I find comfort in the fact that David is still referred to in the Bible as "a man after His [God] own heart." (1 Samuel 13:14 NKJV) It just goes to show that we can mess up badly and still end up well. Like I said before, no one is too far from God's grace. We simply need to do like David in Psalm 51 and offer up to God a broken and repentant heart.

"Let there be tears for what you have done. Let there be sorrow and deep grief. Let there be sadness instead of laughter, and gloom instead of joy. Humble yourselves before the Lord, and he will lift you up in honor."
James 4: 9-10 NLT

We can mess up badly and still end up well.

REVERSE PRIDE

Now that we have a solid understanding of how sin separates us from God and how a repentant heart restores our relationship, I want to talk about something called reverse pride. Most of us understand the danger of pride. Pride is when we put ourselves above God. Our pride convinces us to believe that we are so good on our own that we don't even need God. It's when we think we are too good to need a savior at all. We can even go so far in our pride that we convince ourselves that our sin isn't really sin at all because we have put self on the throne. Well, *reverse pride* is like that but the opposite.

Reverse pride is when we believe that we are too far gone for God's help to reach us. We believe that we are beyond repair for even God. It's still pride because it puts our *circumstances* above God. We replace God on the throne with our pity and our 'poor me' attitude. It keeps us bound to the chains of our problems; and honestly, I think it's a cop-out for facing our mess.

I tried the reverse pride cop-out, too. It didn't work. After a while, it proved to be a miserable place to dwell. Eventually, I had to face the truth that Christ's sacrifice on that cross was bigger than my self-created belief that I was too far gone with a mess too big. The aftermath wasn't going to clean itself up. The wreckage had to be rummaged through, and the lies had to be unveiled. I realized that the only way through this mess was to choose to bring it ALL to God and surrender it.

REFLECTION QUESTIONS:

- Do you believe that your circumstances are too far gone, or do you believe that God can heal you? Why or why not?
- Are there are any areas where you have made your sin part of your identity? Are you willing to let God's Word correct you?
- Do you believe that Jesus died for YOU? Will you accept His gift of forgiveness and salvation?
- Do you want to save your marriage?

CHAPTER 6

✠ ✠ ✠

TO HEAL OR NOT TO HEAL

SINK OR SWIM

When I was around 7 years old, my mom registered my younger brother Chris and I for summer swim lessons at the local pool. Each summer, we would start with the level that followed the level we had completed the previous summer. I couldn't wait to get to the higher levels because that's when I would qualify to jump off the high dive. I was a bit impatient with the process of getting to that high dive, too!

I felt like I spent my first few summers stuck over on the side of the shallow end with all the younger kids who were just trying to blow bubbles out of their noses. Getting through those lower levels seemed to take way too long for me to get to the actual swim technique levels that would lead to the high dive. I don't quite remember why the progression felt so slow. It wasn't like I was ever afraid of the skills or anything. My guess is that I wasn't as strong of a swimmer as I thought. Whatever the reason, I didn't give up. That high dive was worth the hard work for me. I was quite determined to get there!

My younger brother Chris was a whole different story. Chris *hated* summer swim lessons. Maybe it was because he always got dunked by the older kids at the pool, or because he just wasn't motivated by that high dive like me. But for some reason, he just stayed stuck in the lower levels every single summer. I'm not sure he *ever* progressed past bubble-blowing with your nose on the side of the shallow end. And while Chris never progressed past the shallow end in *formal swim lessons*, he got a real-life lesson that taught him a whole lot about swimming in one single day. It was a situation that eliminated his choice to just keep wading in the shallow and forced him to swim in the deep.

My dad had a boat in those same years as summer swim lessons. It was a nice little speed boat for occasional family outings to the lake. My baby brother Brian loved the boat. He was obsessed with the boat. He would sit in the boat while it was parked in our driveway on dry land. He played with toy boats and pointed out every real boat we passed by while driving in the car. He loved riding in the boat and sitting on my dad's lap to help 'drive' the boat. We all loved the boat, too. We all loved trips to the lake with the boat and have fond memories from it. I also have one very formidable memory from that boat.

One summer day, we went out for a day on the lake just like many times before. It was a day just like all the others. The only difference this time was that Chris and I had been taking summer swim lessons for enough years by this point that we should have been able to swim in deep water.

I don't know for sure if my dad knew about my brother's dislike for swim lessons; but I *do* know that he expected both of us to be able to somewhat swim with confidence by then. So midway through the afternoon, he drove the boat into a cove, stopped the engine and anchored in one spot for a while. He jumped out of the boat and started enjoying the cool refreshing water. Then, he invited us to jump in with him. But neither one of us would jump in.

I, for one, did not like murky lake water. I preferred clear chlorinated swimming pool water where I could see the bottom and where fish and snakes did not dwell. I'm still not a big fan of swimming at the lake to this day. So, I politely declined to jump in the lake with my dad. My brother, on the other hand, just flat out refused to jump in. He was so scared to jump into that deep water because he was *convinced* he would sink straight to the bottom. He thought that he hadn't gotten far enough in swim lessons to qualify for deep water swimming and quite frankly, he didn't want to drown. He was quite insistent about NOT jumping into the lake with my dad.

I wish this story ended there. I wish that I could tell you that my dad just left it alone and enjoyed swimming in the lake by himself. I wish I could tell you that Chris and I eventually got sweaty enough sitting in the scorching sun on that hot summer afternoon that we finally pushed past our inhibitions and jumped right in there with my dad. But none of that is how the rest of our day played out.

Nope, my dad didn't take our "no's" as the final answer to his invitation to come swim in the deep lake water with him. After reassuring us that he wouldn't let us drown and trying to convince us that we would be safe to no avail, he climbed back up into the boat and gave us no choice to continue sitting in the boat. He proceeded to throw both of us into the water.

Of course, we both went under, and we both came back up. I came up screaming mad and scared to death that there must be a snake right there in the water beneath me ready to bite me at any second. But I knew how to swim and stay afloat. I didn't panic about being forced to swim. I did what I needed to do to keep myself above the surface but staying angry about being thrown in against my wishes.

However, Chris' reaction was completely different than mine. He instinctually held his breath, blew bubbles out his nose, and floated back to the surface. He continued to tread water while he cried out to my dad in a panic, "I can't swim! Help me! I can't swim!" All the while, he kept treading water and staying above the surface. He was swimming! Even though he *thought* he couldn't swim, he had learned enough in the lower levels of swim lessons to stay afloat and to *not* drown.

And while both of us lived to tell the story of that day, I can't exactly give my dad a parenting award for his method of swim lessons. What I *can* tell you is that I learned an important lesson about life in general from that experience.

I learned that ALL of us have a choice to sink or swim in any given situation. It is always our choice to decide to heal from our wounds, or to choose *not* to heal from our wounds. It is always our choice to heal or to *not* heal from every adversity we experience (or cause). We can sink back from it in fear of what we can't see below the surface, or we can stay afloat and face it even when we can't see it. We can scream all day long that we can't face it or can't heal from it, all the while being completely capable of both. The choice is always ours.

IF NOT FOR MY MARRIAGE, THEN FOR MY SOUL

In the last chapter, I described the process that I had to go through to reach the resolve that I knew God could heal my mess and save my marriage, and that it was *my* choice to *want* to heal. As I stared at that decision face-to-face, my motivation for healing slightly surprised me.

At first, I thought that it was just about healing a broken marriage and saving my family. I could see the damage from the adultery right in front of me. That was the obvious part. It was everything right there on the surface that anybody could point out: a wounded spouse, a possible divorce and broken home, four children to be affected, etc. But it took the Holy Spirit's prompting to show me that I needed to first make the choice to heal for the sake of my *soul*.

Yes, all the surface damage was important and needed healing, too. But this decision had to be made for the sake of the condition of my soul and my relationship with God before I ever started to address the other issues. I had been so close to Him before it all began, yet I had drifted so far away from the Voice of Truth that had once spoken to me. I felt completely numb and detached. Honestly, I believed in that moment that I had been shunned by God. Why? Because I *knew* better than to commit adultery. I couldn't pretend like I accidentally fell into it. I knew that it had been a willful and deliberate choice. And, that part just stabbed me deeply where I was already hurting.

I was so angry at Scott for the part that he had contributed to our marital struggles that I felt betrayed, too. At first, it was just easier for me to put the focus all on him and not look at myself. Like I said before, the adultery happened as a consequence of *both* of our actions. Yes, I am the one who committed the sin; but it was years in the making.

In the years leading up to it, there had been this increasing division in our relationship. He worked a lot and I felt like work mattered more to him than me. I volunteered at church a lot and he felt like my church friends were more important to me than him. The jealousy that was always present caused constant strife. Neither person was putting our spouse first. Neither person was trying to resolve the dissension. Over time, it just became an ugly unspoken existence in our home.

Eventually, I withdrew from a lot of my church activities to try to appease the tension. I had hoped that my being home more often would eliminate the jealousy on his part. But being home all the time was lonely. Since he didn't know how to meet my emotional needs, I had always relied on great friendships to meet them. I have been blessed by very rich, life-giving friendships with wonderful Christian women who encourage and empower one another and hold each other accountable. Without those frequent connections, my soul felt like it was starving and unstable. I had been become an isolated sheep, separated from the flock, and completely vulnerable to the wolf.

In addition to my withdrawal from those groups and friends who kept me accountable, Scott took a second job working nights four nights a week. He left for work very early in the morning and worked very late at night, which meant that I didn't even see him on those 4 days.

There I was, at home all the time with the kids, with very little social connection, with a husband who was working all the time, and with a soul starving for love and affection. I was truly an isolated sheep and the perfect target for the wolf known as Satan. So, when the wolf showed up in the form of a friendly and attractive man who gave me the attention I was craving, I was caught completely off guard and so hungry for relationship that I didn't even see the trap that I was about to get caught up in.

It Started Below the Surface

Did you know that the formation of a cavern happens over hundreds of years under the surface of the earth- long before we even know that it is there? In fact, a lot of caverns go undetected for decades until something happens on the surface above. When that day of discovery happens, many times it's because a sinkhole occurred on the surface. When the sinkhole happens, it can be a small hole beneath, a substantial hole beneath, or a full-blown cavern beneath.

This recently happened in a local neighborhood. A surface sinkhole revealed an entire tunnel system of caverns deep beneath the ground and underneath an existing neighborhood. Houses that had been there for over 30 years had caves underneath them. I'm sure that I would be slightly nervous to discover that the ground deep beneath my home was hollow; but there wasn't anything anyone could do about it.

Fortunately, there ARE things we can do about it when a sinkhole happens in our lives and reveals a giant cavern underneath the surface. That's exactly where I found myself after the adultery. I knew it had started below the surface, and so it had to be addressed below the surface.

Since I shared this story in chapter 4, I want to look at it here again in a deeper context to understand the detached and wounded soul I described earlier in this chapter. I want to fully describe how that process happened, and how I finally woke up from the deception and made the choice to heal.

Step into my shoes for a moment and see if you can identify with any of it. Even if you don't have a similar story, I'm sure that you can find commonalities beneath the external circumstances.

I was a stay-at-home mom of four children, one of whom was severely disabled. I had to forfeit a career that I had worked tremendously hard to achieve because she needed my constant care. Getting my bachelor's degree as a single mom had taken me longer than most people (7 years), so the decision to stay home instead of going to work was a major sacrifice for me. I desired more than anything to be a good mom, so it was a sacrifice that I was willing to make.

Nonetheless, adding two additional kids after our disabled daughter just made my career dream seem even further away. Don't get me wrong- I loved the time at home with my kids. Looking back through the years, I cherish those valuable memories. I loved that time at home with my kids, provided that I still had the ability to connect with friends and the freedom to volunteer at church.

Volunteering gave me a sense of accomplishment and removed some of the void that I felt from not pursuing my career. Being involved with social groups fed my soul's need for relationship. And having a comradery with other stay-at-home moms encouraged me in my purpose as a mother.

Having a husband who worked long hours at a demanding job was hard enough with four kids, especially with one being disabled. So, when he took a second job right after I got uninvolved in so many activities to be at home a lot more, it only perpetuated my beliefs that I was insignificant to him and that he didn't care about our marriage. It was also very counterproductive for dealing with the existing problems.

Enter into the equation the friendly man who shared a lot of commonalities with me. It started out as simple conversation with one another. Harmless interaction. Two people talking with one another on a regular basis and simply enjoying the time spent together. I can't speak for the other person, but I can speak for myself when I say that this relationship fed a very deep longing in my soul. I was starving for intimate connection and conversation. I was so lonely, isolated, and stressed with not much outlet for socializing. So naturally, this relationship became my lifeline for companionship.

Since Scott was working so much, this man quickly became the man who was meeting all my emotional needs that were supposed to be met by my husband. We chatted about all sorts of things during our frequent conversations. He asked me questions about myself and my family. I asked him questions about himself, too. We talked about our lives and our plans for the future. He really listened to me when I spoke, and I believed he cared. I did the same for him. It was innocent and without expectations, until it wasn't.

As many months passed by, it became nearly an entire year of talking together on a regular basis. I believed we had become friends who genuinely enjoyed each other's company. However, my heart started to feel much more than just friendship vibes towards him. My deep-rooted needs for significance and validation were being met by someone of the opposite sex who wasn't my husband.

My soul felt very disconnected from God by this point. Sadly, I started to care less about my mom friends and my church groups. They weren't as important to me as this new relationship that met all my needs. I still attended and served with the family at church on Sundays, but that was the extent of my involvement. I worked a few hours a week in the children's ministry at church, but hardly anyone knew a thing about what was happening in my private life. And even though I tried very hard to ignore any conviction I might have felt, it was looming deep within me.

You see, I knew full well that I was opening a door to the enemy's temptation to sin. Scott and I had attended marriage conferences and intense marriage small groups. We had read all the books and were surrounded by strong Christian couple friends at church who could have kept us accountable. I grew up in church, read the Bible and knew what God said about adultery.

The problem was that I kept everything a secret from everyone. I never discussed how bad our problems were at home. I never told anyone about the pain deep within my soul from feeling insignificant, disregarded and altogether unimportant. I kept all of that under lock and key deep within my heart for no one to know or see.

As I mentioned earlier in the book, I had created the perfect family façade that everyone around us believed. But in reality, that façade was a huge chain of bondage for me. It didn't just keep me dishonest before people, but it kept me dishonest before *God*. Even though I couldn't ignore those deep hurts at the pit of my soul, I didn't dare trust anyone around me with them, much less God. So instead, I just pushed the hurts down deeper, made the decision to feed my screaming flesh, and give in to the sin that was already knocking at my door.

According to www.healthresearchfunding.org, "up to 60% of all spouses will take part in some form of infidelity at least once during their marriage." While this statistic may seem alarmingly high, remember that this number includes *emotional* infidelity, which often goes unreported. However, it is a deceptively innocent form of adultery.

Jesus addressed this is Matthew 5, verses 27-28 NKJV when he said, *"You have heard that it was said to those of old, 'You shall not commit adultery.' But I say to you that whoever looks at a woman in lust for her has already committed adultery with her in his heart."*

Based on the words of Jesus, I should have acknowledged that I was sinning long before the situation further progressed, and I should have turned away as fast as I could. Unfortunately, I continued to believe this deception of innocence.

The day that it evolved into more than just "innocent conversation" is still crystal-clear in my mind. For a long time after everything ended, I replayed that moment over and over again in my head, trying to understand how my soul had strayed so far from God that I didn't seem to give the decision a second thought. It happened on a normal day like any other day. I don't know the answer as to why it happened on *that* day. I guess that I was already so emotionally connected to this person that I had wanted it to happen for a while.

I remember that it didn't even feel wrong in the moment. I had no hesitation about it. I ignored God's still small voice warning me to stop and turn away. It was a critical 'don't open that door' moment and I completely dismissed it. All I recall is that the deception was so strong that I believed that this illusion of a wonderful fulfilling relationship was real. It felt very real. And I'm sad to admit this today, but it felt very good.

I caution you as you read these words. It is not my intent to romanticize this in any way. As I am writing this entire section of this book, I have many friends praying for me. They are praying for me to articulate these words in a way that speaks truthfully to you. My goal is to be as transparent as possible about everything that was happening in my flesh and soul at the time so I can hopefully spare someone else the deep heartache.

It took a long time to break free from the shame and regret that remained long after the adultery had ended. But in the moment, my flesh was much louder and dominant than all the other parts of my being. It was the part being fed the most, so it was the strongest. And my flesh seemed very happy.

However, my soul felt dead and silent. I was distant from God and detached from the body of Christ. I put on a great show of pretend to the people around me who could have helped me if they only knew; but I was living a whole other life in private. I was double-minded. It was both the worst kind of double life and the best kind of double life.

I say that with warning. It was a deceptive form of the best kind of life. Please friend, if you take away nothing else from this book, take away this truth- adultery is deception. It is not real. There's not an argument out there that will convince me otherwise!

Once the adulterous relationship had fully evolved, it intensified the sinful nature inside of me. I was no longer just a pretender who had a great façade. I became a liar to everyone around me. I told so many lies to so many people to cover my tracks and to create opportunities for our next encounter. I became somewhat inattentive to my kids. I still took care of them, of course, but my mind was constantly elsewhere.

Not only was I lying all the time, but I became manipulative. I manipulated everyone around me to get what I wanted. People were simply the means to get what I wanted, and I used them.

The worst part about all of it is that I became totally and utterly detached from Scott in every way. I could lie to his face without even an ounce of guilt. And when his father became deathly ill after undergoing cancer treatment, I was unsympathetic. I pretended like I cared, but it was all an act. I was just cold and callous. His father passed away during that time, yet I remained completely emotionally unavailable to him as he grieved.

There's nothing quite so disheartening as seeing oneself become a completely cold-hearted and mean-spirited person. It was a horrible way to live life because it went completely against the person I used to be. It went completely against the person God had called me to be. I wasn't myself at all.

In the heat of the moment of those adulterous encounters, I loved everything about them. As sad as it is to admit this, my flesh was very happy during that whole period of my life. I can even go so far as to say that my heart felt full because my emotional needs were being met. I eventually fell in love with this person. But the whole time, my soul suffered and died a little more every day.

In church, I would raise my hands in worship, yet feel completely disconnected from God's presence. My soul was so numb. I couldn't hear His voice speaking to my spirit at all. I couldn't connect to Him in prayer- if I even prayed at all. I picked up my Bible from time to time to try to find some sort of justification for what I was doing. Of course, I did not find any such thing.

> *God loves us unconditionally but living His way of life is conditional.*

I was so torn apart. My heart and flesh didn't want to let go of this man and this relationship that felt so right and made me so happy. But my soul longed to be near God, to hear His voice, and to feel His presence again. And no matter how hard I tried, I couldn't have both. God loves us unconditionally but living His way of life is conditional. He says that to follow Him, we must choose to take up our cross and die to our flesh. We can't have our sin and His presence, too.

We can't have our sin and His presence, too.

Willful and deliberate sin does not mesh with a holy and righteous God.

"God has called us to live holy lives, not impure lives. Therefore, anyone who refuses to live by these rules is not disobeying human teaching but is rejecting God, who gives his Holy Spirit to you."
1 Thessalonians 4: 7-8 NLT

It took months for this full-blown adulterous affair to finally come to an end. I couldn't continue living life as a giant phony. God had stayed silent for the majority of that time; or at least I wasn't able to hear Him speaking. Honestly, I wasn't really *trying* to listen, either. I knew that I had completely quenched the presence of the Holy Spirit.

Finally, one night near the end, I woke up in a frantic state of mind. I took a hot bath and then sat on the sofa to read my Bible. I begged God to speak to me. I begged Him to show me what His thoughts were about my adultery (even though I already knew). I begged Him to be near me again. I stopped trying to justify my sin to Him. And I stayed in a state of utter surrender to Him until He finally spoke.

When He started to speak to my spirit, I heard the same still small voice that had warned me not to open that screen door when I was a little girl. It was my loving and concerned Father who didn't want to lose His daughter.

He simply said to my spirit, "Read your Bible."

I opened my Bible to somewhere in the New Testament and started reading the entire thing. At first, everything was just words on a page. Nothing really resonated with me at all. It was as if I was reading a foreign language and I wasn't comprehending anything. I skipped around, trying to find something that spoke to my situation.

The more I read, the more the words started to come alive. Eventually, it felt as if God was speaking right to me. The book of Hebrews resonated the most and spoke the loudest to me. I encourage you to read the entire book on your own. Verses like Hebrews 10: 25-27 cut straight to my heart.

"And let us not neglect our meeting together, as some people do, but encourage one another, especially now that the day of his return is drawing near. Dear friends, if we deliberately continue sinning after we have received knowledge of the truth, there is no longer any sacrifice that will cover these sins. There is only the terrible expectation of God's judgment and the raging fire that will consume his enemies."
Hebrews 10:25-27 NLT

&

"Just think how much worse the punishment will be for those who have trampled on the Son of God, and have treated the blood of the covenant, which made us holy as if it were common and unholy, and **have insulted and disdained the Holy Spirit** *who brings God's mercy to us. For we know the one who said, "I will take revenge. I will pay them back." He also said, "The Lord will judge his own people."*
Hebrew 10:29-30 NLT

I knew at that exact moment that God was lovingly disciplining me, as well as warning me of the severity of my sin.

Those verses told me that:

1. Christ was returning soon, and I didn't want to risk being caught up in sin when he did.
2. My willful and deliberate sin was causing me to reject His redemptive grace.
3. My choice to continue in the sin of adultery was insulting and disdaining the Holy Spirit.
4. I would face God's judgment for my sin if I did not seek forgiveness and repent immediately.

God was **not** speaking lightly to me, but it was because He *loved* me, and it grieved Him to see me so far away from Him. He didn't want to lose me, but He is a Holy and just God. His judgment is fair, and it is from a place of love. God is love. Period.

I knew how serious this moment was for me. God is not someone to be trifled with. We are all sinners who have fallen short of His glory and need a Savior. God is so gracious to us to be willing to provide a way to save us in the first place. He didn't *have* to send Jesus to die in our place. He could have left us in our fallen state without hope. He would have been completely justified in doing so.

Yet, He is so very loving towards us that He couldn't bear to leave us that way. That is why He sent us His very own Son to die the gruesome death that *WE* deserve. And He makes the gift of salvation completely free and available to ALL of humanity who accepts it.

"And just as each person is destined to die once and after that comes judgement, so also Christ was offered once for all time as a sacrifice to take away the sins of many people. He will come again, not to deal with our sins, but to bring salvation to all who are eagerly waiting for him."
Hebrews 9: 27-28 NLT

However, God does not appreciate it when we take His gift of salvation for granted. It grieves Him when we insult the blood of Jesus Christ that was shed for us by continuing in our sinful ways. Salvation is not a license to keep on sinning.

"So we must listen very carefully to the truth we have heard, or we may drift away from it. For the message God delivered through the angels has always stood firm, and every violation of the law and every act of disobedience was punished. So what makes us think we can escape if we ignore this great salvation that was first announced by the Lord Jesus himself and then delivered to us by those who heard him speak?"
Hebrews 2: 1-3 NLT

I know that it is a debatable subject in churchdom as to whether a person can lose their salvation once they've been saved or not. And since I'm not a theological expert, I'm going to leave it at the following statement. My interpretation of Hebrews 10:25-30 that night in my living room was that God was warning ME that my *willful and deliberate* sin was equivalent to walking away from my salvation.

My conviction that night was that I was currently on the path to Hell if I continued to choose my sin over Christ's gift of salvation. I was rejecting God, rejecting His Word, and choosing my eternal destination in Hell *by my own choice.* I believe that this is best defined as apostasy. Apostasy is the act of rejecting one's faith. Because I knew that I was *knowingly* rejecting God's Word about adultery by choosing willful and deliberate sin, I was an apostate.

Just like God had told me to NOT open that screen door as a child, He was telling me in that moment to SLAM that door to the sin that was separating me from Him. I knew right then that it was best not to argue with God Almighty. My eternal destination was certainly NOT worth taking a gamble on. I made the decision that night that the situation HAD to come to an end.

I pray that you make the right decision, too. Rather than debate whether it's possible to reject our salvation, why risk it in the first place? Why take a chance with something so important just because there are some people out there who would argue that it's not possible?

I know I'm not willing to take a chance with *my* salvation and find out in the worst way that I was wrong. Eternity is too important for me. None of those people on either side of that salvation debate are going to be standing beside us to argue on our behalf when we stand before God, anyways. Friend, that's something we need to know for certain!

I must say that **that** night was a defining moment for me! I made my choice without making any excuses. Whatever it would take, I WOULD restore this devastation. I HAD to do it for the sake of my soul! Brother or sister, do it for the sake of your soul!

"So do not throw away this confident trust in the Lord. Remember the great reward it brings you! Patient endurance is what you need now, so that you will continue to do God's will. Then you will receive all that he has promised.

'For in just a little while the Coming One will come and not delay. And my righteous ones will live by faith. But I will take no pleasure in anyone who turns away.'

But we are not like those who turn away from God to their own destruction. We are the faithful ones, whose souls will be saved."
Hebrews 10: 35-39 NLT

REFLECTION QUESTIONS:

- Look beyond the surface-level issues in your life and describe the deeper feelings that you keep hidden. Spend time in prayer to allow God to reveal them to you.
- If you identify with my description of a disconnected soul, what do you need to do to reconnect with God?
- Are you willing to humble yourself to God and admit your sin? If so, will you take the next step of repentance and receive His forgiveness?
- Will you make a commitment to God to completely turn away from areas of willful and deliberate sin in your life?
- Do you choose to begin the healing process?

CHAPTER 7

✠ ✠ ✠

DESERT DECISIONS

GOD'S CHOSEN PEOPLE WERE A LOT LIKE US

I'd like to tell you a little story about God's chosen people, the nation of Israel. It's a very long story that spans through the books of Genesis, Exodus, Leviticus, Numbers, and Deuteronomy. For the sake of time, I'm going to do my best to tell you a very long and powerful story in the most condensed way possible and hope that it all makes sense. Here we go!

Israel was the name God gave to a man named Jacob, the grandson of Abraham. Abraham was an old man who did not have any children. God made a promise to Abraham that he would be the father of many nations and that his descendants would be as numerous as the stars. Abraham was given his son Isaac in his old age, just as God had promised him. Isaac had twin sons, Essau and Jacob. Essau was the oldest; but Jacob tricked Essau out of his firstborn birthright. That's another story, but definitely worth reading on your own.

Jacob grew up and married 2 women who were sisters, Rachel and Leah. Jacob loved Rachel more than Leah. Rachel and Leah's father tricked Jacob into marrying Leah, but he eventually let Jacob marry Rachel, too. Another great story worth reading on your own!

Jacob fathered twelve sons, the four oldest from Leah, the six middle from his two wives' servants, and the two youngest from Rachel. Rachel's firstborn son was Joseph, and he was favored by his father Jacob, which made his ten older brothers jealous. More about that in a minute.

God changed Jacob's name to 'Israel' after Jacob wrestled with God to receive a blessing, and those twelve sons became the patriarchs of the twelve tribes of the nation of Israel. God called Israel His chosen people and promised that He would one day give them a land of their own. God's favor was always on His chosen people. He saved them during a great famine through Jacob's son Joseph.

God had given Joseph the gift of prophetic dreams. After telling his brothers about his dream of them bowing down to him, Joseph was betrayed and sold into slavery in Egypt by his jealous older brothers. Joseph's dream interpretation abilities eventually brought him into a powerful position in Pharoah's palace in Egypt. Joseph's prophetic dreams saved all of Egypt from the disasters of a great famine by telling them in advance to prepare for it. God brought redemption to the family of Jacob, also called Israel, through Joseph's forgiveness and provision towards his brothers during this time of the great famine when they came to Egypt for help. This is yet another great story you should read.

The twelve sons of Israel found favor with Pharoah in Egypt and were invited to stay and live in the land. The people of Israel multiplied and became great in number and mighty in strength in Egypt. The people of Israel stayed in Egypt for 400 years.

Like I said before, this is my very condensed version of what brought Israel to this point in history in the land in Egypt. You can read all of this in its entirety in Genesis chapters 32-50. Trust me, the Bible tells this much better and in greater detail than my super short version. It is rich in content with people with whom we can personally identify.

I will continue with the story in Exodus 1-12.

Four hundred years and generations later after Joseph and his brothers had died, another Pharoah had risen to power who did not know Joseph and the favor that had been bestowed upon his family. This Pharaoh became seriously threatened by Israel's strong presence in the land, fearing that they would turn against him. So, he turned the people of Israel into slaves.

Pharoah oppressed them with crushing labor and did everything he could to destroy their future generations, yet they continued to multiply. And the more they multiplied, the more Pharoah afflicted them with brutal treatment. They were forced to live in complete bondage under crushing harsh labor demands.

Israel cried out to God for deliverance from their oppression in Egypt. God answered their pleas for help by calling on Moses, a Hebrew man himself. Moses had been spared from death as an infant and raised up as a son in Pharoah's house (another great story).

As the infant son of a Hebrew slave woman, his mother knew that Moses was a special child from God. When Pharoah ordered all the infant boys of Israel to be killed, she hid Moses away from Pharoah's men. When it was finally safe to bring him out of hiding, she placed him in a waterproof basket to float to safety down the Nile River. Pharoah's own daughter discovered the infant Moses in the basket in the river and kept him to raise as her own son.

Moses had been raised in Pharoah's house, yet he always knew he was a Hebrew. One day, he saw an Egyptian slave driver beating a Hebrew, so Moses killed the Egyptian. When he found out the next day that his crime had been witnessed by two Hebrew slaves, he ran away and hid in the desert for many years.

It was sometime later while Moses was living in the desert that God appeared to him in a burning bush. God called him forth to be Israel's deliverer from their oppression in Egypt. God sent Moses back to plead with Pharoah to set the people of Israel free.

Pharoah would not honor Moses' plea to let his people go, even after Moses demonstrated God's power through many signs. After Moses went back and forth with Pharoah, God sent nine back-to-back plagues over the land of Egypt. But Pharoah's heart had been hardened and he would not release the people. Finally, God sent one last plague- the death of every firstborn son in Egypt- and Pharoah let the children of Israel go. But, after they had fled Egypt, Pharoah changed his mind and chased after them.

Israel was spared by God from most of the plagues sent to Egypt, including the plague of death of the firstborn son. They safely escaped Egypt and witnessed God's miraculous power yet again when He parted the Red Sea so they could cross over on dry land, escaping Pharoah's approaching army. Then, God caused the sea to crash down on the Egyptian army, killing all of them.

After that, God led them through the desert, appearing as a pillar of cloud in the daytime and a pillar of fire at night, never leaving them alone. His very presence was with them! He brought them to safety and had promised them a land of their own, flowing with milk and honey- The Promised Land.

Despite all the miraculous signs they had just witnessed, the children of Israel complained about Moses and his brother Aaron. I'll pick up in Exodus 16.

"The whole Israelite community set out from Elim and came to the Desert of Sin, which is between Elim and Sinai, on the fifteenth day of the second month after they had come out of Egypt. In the desert the whole community grumbled against Moses and Aaron.

The Israelites said to them, "If only we had died by the Lord's hand in Egypt! There we sat around pots of meat and ate all the food we wanted, but you have brought us into this desert to starve this entire assembly to death."
Exodus 16:1-3 NIV

After hearing their groaning, God told them that He had heard their complaints. He told them He would send them meat that night and bread in the morning. That way, they would know that He was the Lord their God. That evening, He sent quail to cover the camp. And the following morning, God sent down food from Heaven called manna.

Manna was a flaky fine substance that God provided to them every day while they were in the desert. I will talk more about manna in the next chapter. For now, just keep in mind that God provided the manna for them the entire 40 years that they ended up being in the desert.

Up to this point in the story, the Israelites had witnessed the miraculous workings of God so many times that I have a hard time understanding how they could so easily complain. I'll repeat everything they had just experienced once more just so we can get a clear understanding of just how much God had done for them.

Israel had just witnessed God release ten different plagues over the people of Egypt, sparing the Israelites almost every time. They had seen God part the Red Sea completely down the middle and raise up the waters like two walls on each side of them so they could cross it on dry land. Right after they safely crossed over, they witnessed God destroying the Egyptians who chased after them by crashing down the walls of water on top of them. After they escaped the Egyptians, He led them through the desert by *His very presence*. He provided them with water from rocks and food from the sky. He helped them defeat the Amalekites who tried to attack them in the desert. Yet, despite everything God had brought them through, they just continued to do a lot of complaining.

Then the Israelites' complaints and disbelief got even worse! After they had witnessed all that God had just done for them, and they were finally led by Him to the entrance of the Promised Land, they complained again. God instructed them to send in 12 spies to scope out the land for 40 days before they overtook it.

Unfortunately, 10 of the 12 spies came out of the land after the 40 days and spread fear and uncertainty among the people. They spread a bad report to all the people that there were giants in the land and that they looked like grasshoppers in their sight. They affirmed that the land was flowing with milk and honey, but they were convinced that they couldn't fight the giants and win. Once again, they cried and grumbled and wanted to go back to Egypt.

Only two of the spies, Joshua and Caleb, remembered all that God had done and believed that they could defeat the people in their Promised Land. They knew that God would help them, and they trusted His provision.

Unfortunately, no one would listen to them because the other 10 spies spread fear throughout the entire camp. Due to their lack of trust in God *once again*, God told them that they would remain in the desert for 40 years- one year for every day that they had occupied the Promised Land and failed to seize it for their own. This meant that all of that generation would die in the desert and never enter the Promised Land.

Just like the children of Israel in the desert, we can be right in front of *our* Promised Land, but still think that life back in Egypt is better. We can be deceived into believing that the slavery and bondage of our sin is better than our freedom. We can fail to remember everything that God has already brought us through. We can be standing right in front of all His promises of redemption and healing but fail to seize it. We can convince ourselves that it's impossible. We can even spread our disbelief to the people around us. Consequently, we stay stuck in the desert.

> *We can be standing right in front of all God's promises of redemption and healing but fail to seize it.*

Due to listening to the voices of fear and doubt from the ten spies instead of listening to the voices of God's power from Joshua and Caleb, the children of Israel caused their own demise of 40 years sentenced to the desert. God gave us His Word full of the history of His provision and power throughout all of time so that we would trust Him with our own lives. Just like the children of Israel had hundreds of years' worth of stories of God's favor upon them that showed them they could trust Him, we have the same stories to reference when life feels bleak. Our responsibility is to activate our faith through action.

> *Our responsibility is to activate our faith through action.*

DEATH, MIRAGES, OR ABUNDANT LIFE

I believe that in the desert, we can do 1 of 3 things:

1. Lay down, give up, and die of hunger and thirst.
2. Chase after mirages until we die of hunger and thirst.
3. Trust God, do things His way and live an abundant life.

What do each of these things look like in our own lives today? Since I'm talking about a figurative desert, it's important to insert our given circumstances in place of the desert. For me, it was the messy aftermath of the adultery. Not only the mess that I described on the surface, but the spiritual mess in my soul. It went beyond that, too. My very soul was dry and parched.

The desert was where everything that had been brewing in my soul for years was now being brought to light. My Promised Land of healing and redemption was still in front of me. God didn't take it away from me. He is a good Father who wants to give us good things. All His blessings were waiting for me on the narrow road of righteousness. I just had to decide that I wanted to get off my current road leading to destruction. Jesus told us this crucial truth in Matthew chapter 7:

> *"Enter by the narrow gate. For wide is the gate and broad is the road that leads to destruction, and many enter through it. But small is the gate and narrow the road that leads to life, and only a few find it."*
> *Matthew 7: 13-14 NIV*

I needed to come to the realization of the fact that I was on the wrong road. However, my sin had me convinced that I was stuck in the sand of the desert. Consequently, I kept complaining to God about my mess.

Remember when I told you how I went through a period of trying to blame Scott for all of it and not take responsibility for my own part? Well, I eventually got so frustrated with being stuck in such a horrible place that I decided to take responsibility for my part in all of it.

The first option to lie down, give up and die of hunger and thirst is to *choose* to stay stuck. It's basically choosing to claim a victim status and blame all our problems on everyone and everything around us. It's never looking at ourselves and saying, "You know, God, I could use Your help. I've got a lot of bondage in my life that you can help me break free from. Examine me and show me where I need to allow You to work. I don't want to stay on this path of destruction. Help me get back on the narrow road to everlasting life." One of my favorite scriptures to pray to invite God in to look at my heart and help me change directions is found in Psalm 139.

> *"Search me, O God, and know my heart; test me and know my anxious thoughts. Point out anything in me that offends you, and lead me along the path of everlasting life."*
> *Psalm 139: 23-24 NLT*

If I never would have stopped claiming victim status and just chose to stay stuck there in my mess, it would have been a painfully slow death of my soul. Without God's presence in my life, my soul would have died of hunger for God's Word and thirst for God's Truth.

The second option I described is to chase after mirages until we die of hunger and thirst. I believe that a mirage can best be described as anything that is a counterfeit to the Truth of God. This is usually Satan's next best game when we are in the desert. If he (Satan) can present us with something that *looks* like God's provision for us, we might just end up drinking sand, all the while being deceived to think we are drinking water. It's a mirage. It's a counterfeit. It's the enemy's deception. And it leads to death.

> *If Satan can present us with something that looks like God's provision for us, we might just end up drinking sand, all the while being deceived to think we are drinking water.*

My mirage in my desert time was the fantasy I kept telling myself that the adulterous relationship was a real, meaningful relationship that could be blessed by God. I kept telling myself that it was just on pause until we were free to finally be together.

I want to pause right here and comment on that last statement. I am not interested in the stories of how so-and-so knew a couple whose relationship started out in adultery, and they ended up together this way. They may be living in a redeemed situation now and praise God for that! Nevertheless, it was NOT God's will for them to enter a marriage through the sin of adultery. And, if you're reading this right now and happen to be one of those types of couples, I'm not condemning you. Your situation is between you and the Lord. But I *would* advise that you *don't* encourage others to do what you did.

Thirdly, when we are in the desert, there is the last option to trust God, do things His way, and live an abundant life. The key words for me when I made this decision were *surrender* and *obedience*. I would have stayed stuck in that desert for a long time if I hadn't faced the fact that I must surrender to God's will for my life and obey His commands.

You will notice that I talk about surrender and obedience a lot throughout this book. I'll let you in on a secret: it's because I took an unnecessarily long time to grasp these two key factors for living according to God's will. I hope I can spare you some avoidable grief by urging you to implement them now.

My pastor Laura Koke repeatedly emphasized the importance of surrender and obedience in the heart of her messages to women for years. I'm so thankful for her willingness to preach these truths again and again so I wouldn't forget them.

In fact, she emphasized them to me in our personal conversations many times, so I can't deny the fact that I fully knew about them.

I knew these truths, but I just didn't apply them. Real change did not happen for me, and it won't happen for you, until you surrender and obey *completely* to God. Half obedience is still disobedience.

Half obedience is still disobedience.

Surrender is not a bad thing. People tend to think of surrender as the act of giving up. In war, to surrender is to admit defeat. Spiritual surrender is similar but different. It's giving up the sin and lies (fantasies) in our life by laying them down before God. It's admitting that our rebellious way has defeated us. By laying them down, we will no longer fight the war against sin from a place of defeat because God already defeated sin and death on the cross through Jesus. We already have victory when we choose God's way over our own.

Our war was always already won for us. We just need to take ownership of the victory we have already been given.

We may not see anything happening in the physical world where our flesh lives, but victory has already happened in the spiritual world. In our spiritual war, our sin nature must surrender to the sovereign power of God. Our war was always already won for us. We just need to take ownership of the victory we have already been given. I love what the apostle Paul says about this spiritual war:

"We are human, but we don't wage war as humans do. We use God's mighty weapons, not worldly weapons, to knock down the strongholds of human reasoning and to destroy false arguments. We destroy every proud obstacle that keeps people from knowing God. We capture their rebellious thoughts and teach them to obey Christ. And after you have become fully obedient, we will punish everyone who remains disobedient."
    2 Corinthians 10: 4-6 NLT

I especially like that we read the word 'obedience' in this passage. Once we acknowledge before God that our sin, fantasies, and defiant attitudes are wrong, we can make the decision to replace them with the true knowledge of God and begin to walk in obedience. Choosing to walk in obedience was a game changer for me!

For me, walking in obedience meant that I would consciously make the choice to believe God's Word no matter how much my own thoughts, beliefs, and feelings were contrary to it. I would align my life to God's Word instead of trying to align God's Word to my own agenda. No longer would I allow *my* way to dictate my choices. THAT'S how we begin to stay on the narrow road to life!

I am such a firm believer in surrender and obedience that I focused the entire next chapter on the power of choosing Truth over our own desires. But before we end this chapter, I want to leave you with one last thought about getting to the Promised Land from a place in the desert.

THE PROMISED LAND

Imagine planning a big family European vacation. You looked at pictures of all the historic countries of Europe forever, and you are finally ready to see it for yourself. You want the experience and all the emotions that go with it. Everyone around you has taken elaborate trips to Europe and bragged about how fun and exciting it was.

You have already imagined yourself touring all the countries and famous tourist sites: London Bridge, the Queen's Palace, the leaning Tower of Pisa, the gondolas in Venice, the ruins in Rome, etc. Planning your trip was so exciting that you just couldn't wait until the day that you and your whole family boarded that plane and were on your way. You had waited for months for this day, and it was finally here!

You have the time of your life in Europe and create so many fabulous memories. You take amazing photographs of your own to show everyone. You and your family pose at all the famous sites. You eat all the delicious food from various cultures. You finally feel like you have gotten to experience it all for yourself instead of just living vicariously through the experiences of others. It was the most exciting trip of your life. Something your kids will never forget. You can mark it off your bucket list. The joy and satisfaction that you feel is beyond description.

Then, you return home to reality. Life goes right back to the normal mundane routine of things. You share the stories and great pictures of your trip with everyone around you. There was the instant gratification of the trip while you were there, and now there's the remaining gratification every time you tell someone about it. Everything about that trip seems like it was the perfect decision for some excitement in your life, until the day your credit card bill comes in the mail.

No one really knew, except you, that you couldn't actually afford the big European vacation when you first suggested it to the family. But seeing their excitement when you proposed the trip, you just chose to ignore the huge fact that you really couldn't afford it in the first place. You couldn't imagine breaking the bad news to them that the trip was grossly out of your budget when they became so enthusiastically involved with the planning process. So, for the sake of not letting everyone down, you just charged the entire vacation on a credit card. Consequentially, you now had an outstanding balance that was going to take years to pay off.

All in one moment, the thrill of the vacation is completely forgotten because the stress of the debt is now overshadowing all the fun. And you think to yourself, "why, oh, why did I do such a careless thing?!" The mess that you got yourself into can't be reversed! Now, you will have to sacrifice and cut expenses anywhere your budget will allow so that you can start to dig yourself out of the giant financial hole into which you have put yourself. You know it will take years to get back to the financial freedom that you had achieved before this trip, but you don't want to stay in debt forever. In the end, you find yourself questioning whether it was all really worth it.

I used this scenario because I think it's one that we can all relate to in one way or another. It may not be a European vacation, but it could be any number of things. Examples are: purchasing an expensive luxury car rather than a practical commuter car; paying for an Ivy League college education with no scholarships instead of an affordable state university education; planning a grossly overpriced dream wedding rather than a conservative church ceremony; borrowing money for a big house with bonus rooms in a sought-after prestigious neighborhood instead of buying an average affordable home; taking a loan out for a yacht or expensive motorcycle instead of just renting a boat on the lake for a day; or any number of other high-ticket items that none of us actually *need*. Sure, these are fun things to have when we have the money to buy them in the first place. There's nothing wrong with owning any or all of them when we are in a financial position to do so. The problem is when we *want* things that we *can't* afford, and we buy them on credit with an income that can't support the bill.

When we knowingly enter financial debt that we know is above our means, it's financial bondage. The saying goes that the borrower is a slave to the lender. We become slaves to the credit card companies, the banks and the mortgage companies. And we stay slaves to the lenders until we've paid back our debt.

The children of Israel had been slaves to the Egyptians until God brought them out to freedom and to the entrance of the Promised Land. Taking possession of the Promised Land was going to take sacrifice, discipline, and trust in God. When they failed to take possession of the Promised Land the first time they were given the chance, the consequence was that they had to sacrifice by living in the wilderness for 40 years. The wilderness taught them to be disciplined to obey God's commands. And, they had to trust Him to help them when it was time to claim their Promised Land the next time. It wasn't impossible like they claimed.

It's not impossible to get out of debt, either. It just takes sacrifice, discipline, and trust in God's provision. We may have to sacrifice some of the luxuries we once enjoyed for a little while, like cable tv and that fancy gym membership. We will have to discipline ourselves to cook at home instead of stopping at Chick Fil-A every time we crave that dipping sauce (I might be talking to myself here, lol). And we must trust God's provision by believing that He will provide for us while we work our way back to financial freedom.

The Promised Land was promised to the children of Israel long before they were slaves in Egypt. God never cancelled His promise. Their failure to enter it was from their own lack of belief. They put themselves into that 40-year desert detour by their own unwillingness to work for what God was ready to give them. Financial Freedom takes work, too.

Reading about freedom in the context of finances makes it a bit easier to understand it. We can all relate, and we can all agree that it takes work to accomplish it. It's common ground for the average person to discuss and make plans to accomplish.

The same concept applies to reaching freedom in our spiritual lives and gaining possession of our *spiritual* Promised Land. But it's going to take sacrifice, discipline, and trust. We must start by sacrificing our own way of doing things. When we obey God's Word above everything else that tries to dictate our decisions, we begin to walk in spiritual freedom.

When we surrender to God, the result will be freedom from the strongholds of our thoughts and feelings. That's emotional freedom. And when we face the deep-rooted wounds of the past to identify the things that trigger us, we find freedom from all sorts of spiritual and emotional bondage. None of us need to settle for slavery back in Egypt!

I hope that I've inspired you to allow God to search your heart, reveal the things to you that need work, and be willing to surrender them to Him. From there, it's just a matter of obedience to begin seeing the positive changes that will most certainly follow. After all, you are stepping onto the narrow road that leads to everlasting life when you choose obedience. God's blessings of joy and peace are waiting there for you. Let's get to chapter 8 so you can start applying these truths on your road to the Promised Land!

None of us need to settle for slavery back in Egypt!

REFLECTION QUESTIONS:

- What is your 'Egypt?' What is the area of your life that you struggle to leave behind because you are convinced that it is better than the Promised Land in front of you?

- List all the ways you have seen God's faithfulness and provision to you. Put the list somewhere that you can see it often and remind yourself of what God has already brought you through.
- What voices of fear and doubt do you need to silence?
- In your desert, are you ready to choose choice #3: Trust God, do things His way, and live the abundant life?
- Describe what your Promised Land looks like to you.

PART THREE

HERE AND NOW

CHAPTER 8

✠ ✠ ✠

CHOOSING TRUTH

TEXAS WEATHER

I live in the great state of Texas. I've lived here my whole life, so I'm accustomed to conversations that include such fancy expressions as "ya'll" and "fixin' to." And just like Texas has its own dialect, it also has its own weather system, separate from the rest of the country.

In Texas, we can have all four seasons in one day. We can wake up to a nice Spring morning of perfect 70-degree weather, followed by a Hot Summer afternoon of 95-degree sunshine, only to have Fall usher through like a flock of birds migrating south and bring freezing Winter winds that drop the temperatures down to 30 degrees by the time the moon is hung high in the sky and our heads have hit the pillow for the night. It's a common joke on social media memes that Texas is the "bipolar state."

Being a seasoned Texan means that you always pack a pair of shorts *and* a sweater with you, in order to be prepared for whatever the weather may throw at you on any given day. Much like Texas weather, our feelings are so dynamic and ever-changing that they, too, can quickly go from one extreme to the other all in a matter of minutes. Our feelings, if left unchecked, always have the potential to lead us down a path of self-destruction. Just like preparing for Texas weather, we must be prepared for the emotional ups and downs by always packing our minds with the Truth of God's Word.

Our feelings are a very interesting part of the human mind. They are definitely real and can overtake us if we let them. Sometimes, they hit us hard without warning. We can end up on a downward spiral to trouble in no time at all if we allow them to completely dictate our lives. And while they play an important part in understanding our emotional well-being, it's not in our best interests to allow our feelings to be the sole driving force behind our actions.

Don't get me wrong, a healthy emotional gauge is essential to navigate through life's ups and downs. God gave us our feelings on purpose and for a purpose. Our feelings are the indicators to our brain that tell us how to react to various situations. I'm certainly not saying that they should be ignored or disregarded. Rather, our feelings need to be examined and aligned with God's Word before they play a lead role in our reactions and our decision-making process.

THE BREAD OF LIFE

God's Word is the bread of life. Jesus said, "I am the bread of life. Whoever comes to me will never be hungry, and whoever believes in me will never be thirsty." *John 6:35 NIV.* God gave us His son to save us and lead us; and He gave us His Word to guide us in all Truth. Our responsibility is to study God's Word every single day and apply its Truth to our lives. If we don't, we won't be adequately equipped to handle whatever 'weather changes' life throws at us.

I remember when I finally grasped this concept of how essential it was for me to study and apply God's Word every single day. It was yet another lesson learned from God's chosen people. So, let's look at our favorite people in the book of Exodus again. The children of Israel have more to teach us. We will pick up at the part in the story when Moses and the children of Israel had just passed through the Red Sea on their journey to the Promised Land, and the people were beginning to complain to Moses. God responded to Israel's complaints by giving them manna to eat. This time, I'd like to show you a lesson about the manna.

"Then the whole community of Israel set out from Elim and journeyed into the wilderness of Sin, between Elim and Mount Sinai. They arrived there on the fifteenth day of the

second month, one month after leaving the land of Egypt. There, too, the whole community of Israel complained about Moses and Aaron.

"If only the Lord had killed us back in Egypt," they moaned. "There we sat around pots filled with meat and ate all the bread we wanted. But now you have brought us into this wilderness to starve us all to death."

Then the Lord said to Moses, "Look, I'm going to rain down food from heaven for you. Each day the people can go out and pick up as much food as they need for that day. I will test them in this to see whether or not they will follow my instructions. On the sixth day they will gather food, and when they prepare it, there will be twice as much as usual."

So Moses and Aaron said to all the people of Israel, "By evening you will realize it was the Lord who brought you out of the land of Egypt. In the morning you will see the glory of the Lord, because he has heard your complaints, which are against him, not against us. What have we done that you should complain about us?" Then Moses added, "The Lord will give you meat to eat in the evening and bread to satisfy you in the morning, for he has heard all your complaints against him. What have we done? Yes, your complaints are against the Lord, not against us."

Then Moses said to Aaron, "Announce this to the entire community of Israel: 'Present yourselves before the Lord, for he has heard your complaining.'" And as Aaron spoke to the whole community of Israel, they looked out toward the wilderness. There they could see the awesome glory of the Lord in the cloud.

Then the Lord said to Moses, "I have heard the Israelites' complaints. Now tell them, 'In the evening you will have meat to eat, and in the morning you will have all the bread you want. Then you will know that I am the Lord your God.'"

That evening vast numbers of quail flew in and covered the camp. And the next morning the area around the camp was wet with dew. When the dew evaporated, a flaky substance as fine as frost blanketed the ground. The Israelites were puzzled when they saw it. "What is it?" they asked each other. They had no idea what it was.

And Moses told them, "It is the food the Lord has given you to eat. These are the Lord's instructions: Each household should gather as much as it needs. Pick up two quarts for each person in your tent."

So the people of Israel did as they were told. Some gathered a lot, some only a little. But when they measured it out, everyone had just enough. Those who gathered a lot had nothing left over, and those who gathered only a little had enough. Each family had just what it needed.

Then Moses told them, "Do not keep any of it until morning." But some of them didn't listen and kept some of it until morning. But by then it was full of maggots and had a terrible smell. Moses was very angry with them.

After this the people gathered the food morning by morning, each family according to its need. And as the sun became hot, the flakes they had not picked up melted and disappeared. On the sixth day, they gathered twice as much as usual—four quarts for each person instead of two. Then all the leaders of the community came and asked Moses for an explanation. He told them, "This is what the Lord commanded: Tomorrow will be a day of complete rest, a holy Sabbath day set apart for the Lord. So bake or boil as much as you want today, and set aside what is left for tomorrow."

So they put some aside until morning, just as Moses had commanded. And in the morning the leftover food was wholesome and good, without maggots or odor. Moses said, "Eat this food today, for today is a Sabbath day dedicated to the Lord. There will be no food on the ground today. You may gather the food for six days, but the seventh day is the Sabbath. There will be no food on the ground that day."

Some of the people went out anyway on the seventh day, but they found no food. The Lord asked Moses, "How long will these people refuse to obey my commands and instructions? They must realize that the Sabbath is the Lord's gift to you. That is why he gives you a two-day supply on the sixth day, so there will be enough for two days. On the Sabbath day you must each stay in your place. Do not go out to pick up food on the seventh day." So the people did not gather any food on the seventh day.

The Israelites called the food manna. It was white like coriander seed, and it tasted like honey wafers.

Then Moses said, "This is what the Lord has commanded: Fill a two-quart container with manna to preserve it for your descendants. Then later generations will be able to see the food I gave you in the wilderness when I set you free from Egypt."

Moses said to Aaron, "Get a jar and fill it with two quarts of manna. Then put it in a sacred place before the Lord to preserve it for all future generations." Aaron did just as the Lord had commanded Moses. He eventually placed it in the Ark of the Covenant—in front of the stone tablets inscribed with the terms of the covenant. So the people of Israel ate manna for forty years until they arrived at the land where they would settle. They ate manna until they came to the border of the land of Canaan."

Exodus 16:1-35 NLT

This story is just rich with substance and detail. There is so much we can take away from it. God was teaching Israel to trust His *provision* in the desert. He was also teaching them to trust His provision *one day at a time.* He taught them that they couldn't store up extra manna for an extra day because it would rot and attract maggots- except for the day before the Sabbath. The manna on the sixth day was perfectly designed to not rot or attract maggots when they gathered enough of it for two days. It was the only day of the week that God specifically told them to gather a 2-day supply in order to rest on the Sabbath.

We need Jesus every single day!

While this may seem like a lot of rules for Israel to follow just to be able to eat, God was teaching them so much more than to merely follow rules for the sake of following rules. He was teaching them *trust and dependence.* He was teaching them that they needed Him *every single day.* They couldn't gather manna for two days during the week because they had to learn to trust Him to provide it for them each new day. They were learning a *daily dependence* on God's perfect provision. They were learning that they could trust *Him alone* to meet their needs. And they learned that they needed to *rest* on the Sabbath just like God rested on the seventh day of creation.

God's Word is our manna. We need to read and digest His Word every single day. Just like the manna, we can't store it up to last for days at a time. We can't just go to church on Sunday and hear a message that we expect to carry us for the whole week. We can't call it 'Bible study' when other Christians share a scripture on social media that we come across while scrolling and click 'like.' We can't read our Bible on Monday and call it our 'fill up' for the whole week. Our spirit isn't a gas tank that only needs filled every once in a while when we are on empty.

> *Our spirit isn't a gas tank that only needs filled every once in a while when we are on empty.*

We also can't think that spending an hour and a half with God on Sunday at church is going to create a rich relationship with Him. A rich relationship is built through quality time and frequent interaction. It's also personal. It's not based on someone else's experience that they share with us. We must have our own personal walk with God.

Jesus taught us to pray The Lord's Prayer (Matthew 6:9-13 NKJV), which includes the part that says, "give us this day our *daily bread.*" And Jesus said, "I am the bread of life" (John 6:35 NLT). When we understand our need for Him every single day that we wake up with another day of breath in our lungs, we grow into a daily dependence of His provision- and His provision alone. We start to crave time with Him and seek His Word throughout the day to help us navigate every situation we face. We stop relying on ourselves and our feelings for the answers because He really *does* equip us with an answer for every question.

Our spirit operates as a vessel that He constantly pours *through.* We aren't designed like a gas tank that just gets filled up when we are on empty. We are designed as a vessel of God that He uses to pour *in* and *through* to a lost and broken world. We are just the vessel. He is the substance. And His Word is the fuel- a fuel that must be constantly replenished on a daily basis.

When we try to store up His Word all at one time, we are left with rot and maggots.

Now, don't get me wrong. It is powerful to memorize scripture and keep God's Word stored in your mind. The Word is a weapon against the ploys of the enemy, and it is a powerful tool for shutting down his lies. But there's something very different about going to God and His Word as our approach to *each new day.*

Something special happens in the daily quiet time with God. Nine times out of ten, my scripture reading for the day will be exactly timed for something I will face that day. And when I have rushed out the door without spending time with God that morning, I always seem to encounter an adverse situation that I am completely ill-equipped to face. I feel dry and empty and without guidance. Then, later in the day when I get a chance to read my Bible, I'm not kidding you- there will be the answer that I needed all along. I kick myself every time because I could have avoided the stress of the situation if I had just been equipped- if I had just made the time for Him in the beginning.

Entering the day without praying and equipping yourself with God's Word is like that bad dream we all have as kids that we showed up to school in our pajamas, or worse- naked. I remember having that dream a couple of times. I'm glad it never actually happened. Yet, we show up to life spiritually naked when we don't dress ourselves in God's Word every day.

We show up to life spiritually naked when we don't dress ourselves in God's Word every day.

Our spirits have a hunger that can't be satisfied with anything else. The manna of God's Word dresses us AND feeds us.

All fresh food eventually rots. Sure, you can buy that freeze-dried astronaut food if that stuff suits you. But I can't imagine eating astronaut food every single day. I want a farm-fresh scrambled egg with a fresh avocado and a piece of toast for breakfast.

The manna was fresh; but it wasn't anything spectacular. They called it 'manna' because manna means 'what is it?' They couldn't exactly explain what it was; but it satisfied their appetites and sustained them. And it was freshly supplied by God himself every day.

My favorite part is how the manna they gathered on the sixth day *didn't* rot or attract maggots overnight like it would all the other days. No, it was specifically designed by God to stay fresh for two days so that the people could rest on the Sabbath. God gave them the gift of the Sabbath as a day to rest. And He showed them that He would provide for their need for rest just as importantly as their need for food. God is just perfect like that.

Just like God provided for Israel's need for rest, He will multiply back to us the time that we commit to pray and read our Bibles every day. So, we don't need to use the excuse that we don't have enough time. By trusting Him with the first minutes of our time each day, He will provide us with the exact time we need to accomplish our goals for the day, as long as they are in step with His plans for us. When we use the excuse of not having enough time to start our day with Him, we are *really saying* that we don't completely trust God *with* our time. That's absurd considering that He is the creator of time itself. And He is the author of each day of life that we are given. So why would we struggle to trust the Giver of the gift with the gift itself?

> *Why would we struggle to trust the*
> *Giver of the gift with the gift itself?*

CORRECT APPLICATION

One of Israel's biggest issues with God's instructions was following them *correctly*. Even after He told them NOT to gather more than enough manna for one day, some of the people did it anyways. And their manna turned to rot and attracted maggots. Still, other people went out to gather manna on the Sabbath when God had specifically told them not to gather on the Sabbath but to rest. Why was it so hard to follow the specific instructions of the God of the universe who was supplying their every need? I wonder the same thing about myself.

Even though I know that spending time with God and praying throughout the day will lead me in a beautiful life of fellowship and freedom, I will still allow my need for control to take over. And I will still let my feelings control my decisions instead of seeking God in the moment. I don't know why I do this when I've got God Almighty perfectly preparing me, equipping me, and walking with me into every day when I *just ask*. He says in Luke 11: 9-10 (NLT):

"And so I tell you, keep on asking, and you will receive what you ask for. Keep on seeking, and you will find. Keep on knocking, and the door will be opened to you. For everyone who asks, receives. Everyone who seeks, finds. And to everyone who knocks, the door will be opened."
Luke 11: 9-10 NLT

Why would anyone want to mess up such a perfect and promising gift? I don't know what was going through the minds of the people of Israel when they gathered more manna than they needed or when they tried to gather on the Sabbath; but I know that I have done the same thing in a different way. I have failed to follow His instructions correctly and I have failed to trust His Word completely. How blessed we are to have a Heavenly Father who is so patient with us!

TOTAL IMMERSION

Now that we've established the fact that Jesus is the bread of life, that God's Word is our daily manna and that we must follow His instructions correctly, let's talk about following God's Word completely. I'm calling this 'total immersion.' There are three definitions of immersion that I want to apply to this idea of total immersion.

IMMERSION

Immersion- The act of immersing or the state of being immersed, such as:

a) absorbing involvement (such as politics)
b) instruction based on extensive exposure to surroundings or conditions that are native or pertinent to the object of study (such as a foreign language)
c) baptism by complete submersion of the person in water

(www.Merriam-webster.com)

First of all, we must be completely immersed in God's Word and in our relationship with Him. Our entire life should be involved in daily communion with our Heavenly Father. We should become so absorbed in God's presence that our very being exists to magnify His name. Because well, that is why we were created. He created us for fellowship with Him. We are His children, and He wants to spend time with us.

Secondly, we must be immersed in the Word of God and in our relationship with Him as if we were trying to become fluent in a foreign language. I've heard that the best way to learn a foreign language is to be immersed in the country and culture of the language you're trying to learn. I can personally attest that, after taking Spanish Language for two years in high school and four semesters in college, my fluency is lacking in a way that a person who has been immersed in the spanish-speaking culture isn't lacking. Immersion is more effective. We must approach God's Word the same way. When it feels like a foreign language to us, we need to apply ourselves to extensive exposure to it until it becomes our native tongue.

Lastly, we must be immersed in the Word of God and in our relationship with Him by being fully submerged like in water. Go completely under and be fully covered in His Word leaving nothing dry! We need to wash ourselves in Truth- every part of us- seen AND hidden. It is imperative that we ask Jesus to cleanse us of the falsehoods and lies that we so strongly believe. The Holy Spirit should guide us. It is fundamental that we are governed by Truth and love, even when it goes against our feelings and the desires of our flesh.

"So I say, walk by the Spirit, and you will not gratify the desires of the flesh. For the flesh desires what is contrary to the Spirit, and the Spirit what is contrary to the flesh. They are in conflict with each other, so that you are not to do whatever you want."
Galatians 5: 16-17 NIV

By immersing in this Truth as the way we live, we can demolish the temptations of our sinful desires and deceitful feelings. These prideful seductions are guaranteed to romance us with fantasies of a life without God that are FAR from reality.

*"We demolish arguments and every pretension that sets
itself up against the knowledge of God, and we take captive
every thought to make it obedient to Christ."*
2 Corinthians 10:5 NIV

We can't spiritualize our sin into righteousness. What's right
is right and what's wrong is wrong. No exceptions. Just because it
feels right doesn't mean that it *is* right. Of course, we need to *read*
God's Word and be immersed in it to know what God says is right
and wrong in the first place. And when we become aware of a sin in
our life, no matter how much we like it and it feels natural and good
to us, it must go. It can't be mixed in with the Truth.

> *Just because it feels right doesn't
> mean that it is right.*

It's like oil and water. Have you ever done that elementary
science experiment where you mix vegetable oil in a bottle with
water? Then, you pass it around the room, and everyone shakes it
as hard as they can to try to mix the two contrasting substances. But
no matter how much it is shaken, the two substances just won't mix.

Sin and righteousness are like oil and water. If we get fully
immersed in God's Word and His way of life for us, but we try to bring
our sin along with us, it's like oil in the living water of God. It won't mix.
It will keep us at constant odds with ourselves, with both our spirit
and our flesh battling for control, just like we read in Galatians 5:17.

We can certainly relate to the apostle Paul's battle with the sinful
nature:

*"And I know that nothing good lives in me, that is, in my
sinful nature. I want to do what is right, but I can't. I want to
do what is good, but I don't. I don't want to do what is wrong,
but I do it anyway. But if I do what I don't want to do, I am not
really the one doing wrong; it is sin living in me that does it.*

*I have discovered this principle of life—that when I want
to do what is right, I inevitably do what is wrong. I love God's
law with all my heart. But there is another power within me*

that is at war with my mind. This power makes me a slave to the sin that is still within me. Oh, what a miserable person I am! Who will free me from this life that is dominated by sin and death? Thank God! The answer is in Jesus Christ our Lord. So you see how it is: In my mind I really want to obey God's law, but because of my sinful nature I am a slave to sin."
Romans 7:18-25 NLT

I find it reassuring that *even the great apostle Paul* struggled with the internal battle of sin versus righteousness. And I find greater comfort in the fact that God sent Jesus Christ to die for all of us so that we could have the Holy Spirit to help us. I'm going to pick up with the same scripture, but switch to The Message paraphrase:

"I've tried everything, and nothing helps. I'm at the end of my rope. Is there no one who can do anything for me? Isn't that the real question?
The answer, thank God, is that Jesus Christ can and does. He acted to set things right in this life of contradictions where I want to serve God with all my heart and mind but am pulled by the influence of sin to do something totally different."
Romans 7:24-25 MSG

I must warn you, though! Be careful NOT to use this scripture as an excuse to justify our sinful natures! Like Paul, we need to continue to seek God's help to overcome the sin that is at odds with the spirit within us. Our feelings must come under God's authority, too.

I said this earlier in the book, and I'll say it again because it's worth repeating. There's no "My Feelings Exception Clause" to the Truth of God's Word. Most times, our feelings are fed by our sin nature. And we can truly convince ourselves that God will make an exception for our feelings and for our sin of choice. We want to get our way and believe that God just wants us to be happy. We hear phrases in the world that tell us: "just follow your heart" and "just do what feels right." I'm not going to beat around the bush about this. These are big huge lies! They are traps of the enemy to lure us away from Truth. The Bible says that:

"The human heart is the most deceitful of all things, and desperately wicked. Who really knows how bad it is? But I, the Lord, search all hearts and examine secret motives. I give all people their due rewards, according to what their actions deserve."
Jeremiah 17: 9-10 NLT

&

"It is obvious what kind of life develops out of trying to get your own way all the time: repetitive, loveless, cheap sex; a stinking accumulation of mental and emotional garbage; frenzied and joyless grabs for happiness; trinket gods; magic-show religion; paranoid loneliness; cutthroat competition; all-consuming-yet-never-satisfied wants; a brutal temper; an impotence to love or be loved; divided homes and divided lives; small-minded and lopsided pursuits; the vicious habit of depersonalizing everyone into a rival; uncontrolled and uncontrollable addictions; ugly parodies of community. I could go on. This isn't the first time I have warned you, you know. If you use your freedom this way, you will not inherit God's kingdom."
Galatians 5:19-21 MSG

That's a serious warning at the end of this passage from Galatians 5! Our inheritance of God's Kingdom is at stake. I don't know about you, but I'm not willing to risk my eternal salvation on something that my *feelings* told me I needed more than a righteous life with Christ and an inheritance of His kingdom! Eternity is forever. Why take a chance with something so important for a fleeting pleasure in this life?

> *There's no "My Feelings Exception Clause" to the Truth of God's Word.*

Furthermore, we certainly can't let society tell us what is right from wrong, because society is forever changing the rules to fit the most current and popular agenda. Whatever chosen sin has been made acceptable these days gets a new set of rules, re-written to include that sin in the club. In current times, some of these sins are celebrated with parades, clubs, entertainment venues, and holidays dedicated to them. Society has created entire movements behind these acceptable sins, choosing to completely ignore and disregard God's Word. And God knew all along that this would happen, starting with people in the church:

"For a time is coming when people will no longer listen to sound and wholesome teaching. They will follow their own desires and will look for teachers who will tell them whatever their itching ears want to hear. They will reject the truth and chase after myths."
2 Timothy 4:3-4 NLT

I can personally attest to living my life this way. In the middle of my sin of adultery, I tried to justify it, too. As I said in an earlier chapter, I gathered people around me who accepted it and celebrated the juicy details of it. I tried to justify it by manipulating God's word, too.

I tried to convince myself that God wanted me to be happy because He loves me. But the truth is that God wanted me to be *holy* because He loves me. Holiness trumps happiness. Holiness is eternal. Happiness is fleeting. Holiness enters the kingdom of Heaven. Happiness is a self-centered ticket to a ride on the broad path to destruction and eternity in Hell.

"You can enter God's Kingdom only through the narrow gate. The highway to hell is broad, and its gate is wide for many who choose that way. But the gateway to life is narrow and the road is difficult, and only a few ever find it."
Matthew 7:13-14 NLT

Jesus said those words in Matthew 7. He said that *many* people choose the broad path. That tells me that, just because the majority says something is acceptable, doesn't make it right. Because the majority is the "many." According to Jesus, the majority of people are choosing the broad path to hell and only a few people are choosing the narrow path to everlasting life. Since that's the case, wouldn't you rather be in the "few" category? Don't you want to be on that narrow road? Well, here's good news: you can!

> *"This High Priest of ours understands our weaknesses, for he faced all of the same testings we do, yet he did no sin. So let us come boldly to the throne of our gracious God. There we will receive his mercy, and we will find grace to help us when we need it most."*
> *Hebrews 4: 15-16 NLT*

Praise God for help and hope in Jesus Christ! We aren't left without a way off our broad road approach to life. God knew the risk He took when He gave us free will. He saw mankind use free will to choose sin ever since the beginning with Eve's choice in the Garden. And He sent Jesus to save us from our own destruction. All we must do is choose Truth and choose to receive help from the Holy Spirit. The life that we are promised when we make this choice is beautiful.

> *"But the Holy Spirit produces this kind if fruit in our lives: love, joy, peace, patience, kindness, goodness, faithfulness, gentleness, and self-control. There is no law against these things!*
> *Those who belong to Christ Jesus have nailed the passions and desires of their sinful nature to his cross and crucified them there."*
> *Galatians 5:22-24 NLT*

And, here's the Message paraphrase:

> *"But what happens when we live God's way? He brings gifts into our lives, much the same way that fruit appears in an orchard—things like affection for others, exuberance about life, serenity. We develop a willingness to stick with things, a sense of compassion in the heart, and a conviction that a basic holiness permeates things and people. We find ourselves involved in loyal commitments, not needing to force our way in life, able to marshal and direct our energies wisely. Legalism is helpless in bringing this about; it only gets in the way. Among those who belong to Christ, everything*

connected with getting our own way and mindlessly responding to what everyone else calls necessities is killed off for good—crucified."
Galatians 5:22-23 MSG

TAKE EVERY THOUGHT CAPTIVE

How do we start living this life of choosing to be led by the Holy Spirit and Truth? It starts by taking every thought (and feeling) captive and making them obedient to Christ. What I mean by that is that we take our sinful thoughts and feelings, and we replace them with God's Word. We don't allow them to hold a place in our minds. Instead, we put God's Word into every spot where sinful thoughts once took up residence.

Also, we stop listening to the lies of the world around us. We don't turn to our ever-changing society as our compass for right and wrong. We acknowledge that society doesn't want to help us. Society just wants to pull us down with them on their already sinking boat. The Message paraphrase describes society perfectly here:

"The world is unprincipled. It's dog-eat-dog out there! The world doesn't fight fair. But we don't live or fight our battles that way—never have and never will. The tools of our trade aren't for marketing or manipulation, but they are for demolishing that entire massively corrupt culture. We use our powerful God-tools for smashing warped philosophies, tearing down barriers erected against the truth of God, fitting every loose thought and emotion and impulse into the structure of life shaped by Christ. Our tools are ready at hand for clearing the ground of every obstruction and building lives of obedience into maturity."
2 Corinthians 10:3-6 MSG

Society teaches a self-centered mentality. It's all about making ourselves happy and being true to ourselves, no matter how contrary to God's Word our 'true' selves might become. Sadly, society's way of life drives us further from God's way of life for us. If we are not careful, before we know it, we can get so comfortable with our sin nature that it becomes our very identity. Society has already decided that it's okay to base our identity on our sinful choices. And yet, it's completely contrary to the Truth that sets us truly free. We have already been warned that those that live this way will not inherit the Kingdom of Heaven!

> *If we are not careful, before we know it, we can get so comfortable with our sin nature that it becomes our very identity.*

Negative thoughts are another way to drive us further away from Truth. Negative thoughts are like weeds in a garden. Sure, one weed might not hurt your flowers too much. But that weed will multiply, eventually choking out the flowers until they are dead. Just like a single weed is deceptively unthreatening in a garden, a single negative thought is a deceptive force growing in your mind.

If a deceptive thought is not addressed, removed, and replaced with the Truth of the Word of God, it will eventually multiply until it overtakes your mind with lies and wrongful thinking, choking out whatever Truth you *did* possess. And the ultimate price you pay is death of your joy, hope and peace.

As I think about negative thoughts as weeds in a garden that we must uproot before they take over, I am reminded of a recent weather phenomenon that we had here in Texas.

It started a few days before Valentine's Day. The air dropped to an unusually cold temperature for this area- and it *stayed* cold! Normally, it will just drop to a below-freezing temperature for a day or so, and then bounce right back up to the milder range that we are used to having. Well, this February temperature drop brought with it a massive ice storm that blanketed the roads, ground, and plants with a thick sheet of ice that did not melt for a week! A week of freezing temperatures in Central Texas just does not happen. And many of our plants and trees just couldn't withstand the unrelenting cold.

Trees started snapping off from the weight of the ice. Many of the smaller and less hearty trees snapped and broke within the first few hours of the ice storm. Other larger trees managed to withstand a little while longer before they eventually started snapping, too.

Some trees even snapped right off at the top! It was an eerie sound to hear from inside the shelter of our homes, many without electricity or heat. People described the snapping branches as sounding like gunshots, and the thud of a giant branch onto the ground or a roof sounding like thunder.

Yet, in the midst of all of the snapping trees, some trees stood perfectly intact, not a single branch broken. I'm going to tell you about 2 particular trees that held their frames strong amidst this freeze phenomenon being referred to as the "Snowpocolypse of 2021."

The first tree is a huge oak tree that stands at the top of the hill of my neighborhood that used to be a ranch before it was a subdivision. That old oak tree is planted near the original ranch house that still stands in its place on the hill today. I'm guessing that it's over 100 years old because it is enormous! And being that old means that it has most certainly withstood other storms and weather phenomenon in the past.

As soon as the first wave of the ice storm had covered everything in the area in a thick sheet of heavy frozen water, I drove up to the ranch house to check on that old oak tree. Thankfully, I found it to be perfectly fine. Its long, majestic branches were heavily weighted down to the point that some of them were touching the ground. But the strong branches that sprouted right from the trunk of the tree were sufficiently sturdy, yet flexible enough, to hold up to the weight of the ice while adequately bending to the support from the ground below. Throughout the entire week of the freeze, that tree never buckled under the weight of the ice. Not a single branch broke off. And it went right back to its stately form after the storm.

The second tree is the tree in my front yard that we used to call "the ugly tree." For some reason, this tree had always looked spooky by the way it grew so oddly. One time, it got extremely tall, looking like two separate trees on top of each other, with scraggly branches growing out on the sides all over the place. We tried to prune it several times to make it rounder, but it just grew right back "ugly" the next year. Finally, one Fall after all the leaves had fallen off, I got this idea to completely cut off the top of the tree and prune that hideous thing back to practically nothing.

I laugh as I think back to the year we butchered that "ugly tree." Our neighbors questioned our decision to cut it off at the top. Consequently, it was an eyesore for the entire winter that followed. But Spring! When Spring finally rolled around and the branches started budding new leaves, our "ugly tree" blossomed into a perfectly round and full shade-bearing beautiful tree! My outrageous plan had worked.

During the "Snowpocolypse of 2021," our "beautiful ugly tree" sparkled with that thick coat of ice that covered all its bare branches, not a one of them being overly weighted down by the ice. And while trees were snapping all around it, it never budged. It held strong throughout that whole week just like it's 100-year-old cousin tree up the hill at the ranch house.

Both trees withstood the test of that storm, but for very different reasons. The old oak tree stood strong during that phenomenon for two reasons: it had weathered other storms and its roots had grown deep. Certainly, that old oak tree had survived other storms over the past 100-plus years. Each time it survived a storm, its branches endured resistance from an external force that caused them to get stronger and stronger. Thus, this ice storm was nothing but another storm that hardly even threatened the old oak tree. It came, it brought adversity, and it left, hardly making a mark on that tree.

Secondly, the old oak tree had deep roots. It wasn't only being nourished by the sun above and the periodic rainfall; but it was being nourished by the nutrients and water deep below the surface where other trees had yet to reach. As a result, the ice on the outside of the branches had little effect on the powerful force of nature that was happening on the inside, going all the way down to those deep roots.

Just like that old oak tree, we can become so deep-rooted in Truth that the external forces of sin can't shake us. Just like that tree, society's ever-changing philosophies will come and go like a storm, but we will remain steadfast.

"Let your roots grow down into him, and let your lives be built on him. Then your faith will grow strong in the truth you were taught, and you will overflow with thankfulness.

Don't let anyone capture you with empty philosophies and high-sounding nonsense that come from human thinking and from the spiritual powers of this world, rather than from Christ. For in Christ lives all the fullness of God in a human body. So, you also are complete through your union with Christ, who is the head over every ruler and authority."
Colossians 2: 7-10 NLT

When we are rooted and grounded in Christ, we can be like that old oak tree, weathering the storms of life with grace and strength. I know that's how I want to live! Even if everyone around me is snapping under pressure, I want to be so rooted and nourished by the Truth of God's Word that I don't break with all the others. We may not live as many years as the old oak tree, but the Truth with which we determine to align our lives will pour over into the generations that follow. We have the power to change the trajectory for our children's children precisely by choosing to be rooted in the Truth!

Now, back to the "beautiful ugly tree." That tree taught me an important lesson about the necessity of pruning. Fortunately for our tree, the evidence of its ugliness was on the outside for everyone to see. There was no hiding the fact that it needed some work. The external evidence made it an easy choice to prune what needed to go.

Unfortunately for us humans, our need for pruning is NOT always evident on the outside. We can hide the things that need to be pruned out of our lives. We can look much like all the other trees around us, and no one will know that we've got some stuff that needs to go- until a storm comes along and sits on us for much longer than we can withstand. At that point, we will be exposed at our areas of weakness as we snap under the weight of adversity.

But praise God we absolutely have a choice to prune our stuff with His help before a storm comes along and does it for us! By choosing Truth, we can prune the lies and the negative thoughts when we become aware of them. And we become aware of them by learning the truth in the Bible. Each time we encounter a Truth that is contrary to our wrong belief, we must choose to prune away the wrong belief. As we do this, our branches of Truth become so strong that we will glisten with beauty right in the middle of a storm.

> *We can look much like all the other trees around us, and no one will know that we've got some stuff that needs to go- until a storm comes along and sits on us for much longer than we can withstand.*

However, just like the trees that snapped all around my "beautiful ugly tree," if we don't do the pruning, God will do it for us. Jesus said:

"I am the true vine, and my Father is the gardener. He cuts off every branch in me that bears no fruit, while every branch that does bear fruit he prunes so that it will be even more fruitful. You are already clean because of the word I have spoken to you. Remain in me, as I also remain in you. No branch can bear fruit by itself; it must remain in the vine. Neither can you bear fruit unless you remain in me.

"I am the vine; you are the branches. If you remain in me and I in you, you will bear much fruit; apart from me you can do nothing. If you do not remain in me, you are like a branch that is thrown away and withers; such branches are picked up, thrown into the fire and burned."
John 15:1-6 NIV

That tree of mine didn't snap in the storm because we had pruned it when it needed pruning. The top of that tree would have most likely snapped off like so many of the other trees if we hadn't cut it off when needed. By removing it when we did, the remaining parts of the tree were able to grow stronger. The energy of the tree became more focused on the *living* parts of the tree.

When we remove the wrong thoughts from our minds, the *Truth* will grow stronger. When the lies of sin and shame and negative thoughts get pruned away, the Truth that remains in us gets stronger and more beautiful. We, too, can be a "beautiful ugly tree" if we just let the ugly go. Our lives will also become more fruitful.

Taking our thoughts captive and making them obedient to God's Word is always our choice, though. If we don't come to the place of resolve where we *decide* that we will choose Truth over everything else, we can stay stuck for years. We must be so desperate for God's will for our lives that we won't settle for anything outside of that. Don't wait for a storm to make the decision *for* you!

REFLECTION QUESTIONS:

- What wrong thoughts do you need to remove from your mind? Are you willing to take them captive and make them obedient to God's Word, regardless of the cost to your own desires?
- Do you identify any "my feelings exception clauses" in your own life? Are you willing to acknowledge that they are contrary to God's will for your life and to repent from them?
- Are you ready to stop being stuck?
- Make a list of those sinful thoughts, feelings and 'exception clauses' that you've allowed to remain in your life and nail them to the cross today!

CHAPTER 9

— ✠ ✠ ✠ —

THE DAILY SURRENDER

LIVE AND LEARN

I'm what I call a 'live and learn kid.' I was rarely the kid who would have ever listened to those 'don't open that door' moments at all. I admit that I most certainly would have eaten the forbidden fruit in Eden, too. I have managed to learn the hard way more often than doing it right the first time.

I have two of those 'live and learn kids' of my own, now. My four children are spread out over 12 years. My oldest daughter Morgan was 12 when my only son and the baby of the family, Clay, was born.

In the middle are my two other daughters, Anna and Sarah. Those two have always been my 'grace in the middle kids.' With Anna being born with a disability, she couldn't have disobeyed me if she had wanted due to her limited physical abilities. And Sarah is the child that just does what she's told. I don't have to nag her about homework or chores. Well, most chores. She can procrastinate about unloading the clean dishes from the dishwasher until both sides of the sink are completely full of dirty dishes and I must 'gently' remind her to do it again. Thankfully, unplugging the Wifi router that shuts down her internet is the "gentle reminder" that can move her to action very quickly!

On the other hand, the other two kids- Morgan and the one and only son Clay- they don't just do things because they are *told* to do them. On the contrary, they do things only when there's a fire put under their bottoms to move them to action, be it a threat of discipline or a hard-learned consequence.

I AM happy to report that Morgan is now fully grown and married with kids of her own and she did eventually grow out of this, but not my son. I'm in the thick of it with him and his 15-year-old 'I know everything' attitude. Fortunately for me, I'm a bit wiser this time around, having raised three more before him. So far, he hasn't gotten away with nearly as much stuff as Morgan did.

The most comical part about all of this is that I can't even get angry or question why these two kids have been so hard because I know *exactly* why they act like they do. They are their mother's children. And, they have given me a good dose of what it must feel like to be my Heavenly Father who has had *me* for a child for all my years.

I am most certainly one of His 'live-and-learn kids' who just recently concluded that it is most reasonable to read and believe my Bible, trust that God really does know what's best for me (even when I don't like it) and obey Him no matter what. There's so much more peace in my life now that I live this way. Life is not any easier. It's just that God gives me peace for every circumstance.

Assuredly, this decision to simply be obedient didn't come easily or without consequences of all kinds before I was finally broken and humble enough to admit that I really didn't know everything like I claimed. The Message paraphrase sums it up quite well:

> *"And so I insist—and God backs me up on this—that there be no going along with the crowd, the empty-headed, mindless crowd. They've refused for so long to deal with God that they've lost touch not only with God but with reality itself. They can't think straight anymore. Feeling no pain, they let themselves go in sexual obsession, addicted to every sort of perversion.*
> *But that's no life for you. You learned Christ! My assumption is that you have paid careful attention to him, been well instructed in the truth precisely as we have it in Jesus. Since, then, we do not have the excuse of ignorance, everything—and I do mean everything—connected with that old way of life has to go. It's rotten through and through. Get rid of it! And then take on an entirely new way of*

life—a God-fashioned life, a life renewed from the inside and working itself into your conduct as God accurately reproduces his character in you."
Ephesians 4:17-24 MSG

I started my restoration journey when I surrendered this story to print. Believe me, it's much easier to tell people about how God has worked in our lives through difficult seasons or various trials when we are not the ones at fault. It's much easier to talk about how we overcame suffering with God walking beside us when we are not to blame for the cause of our suffering. It's NOT easy to tell people about OUR sin and OUR wrongdoings and how WE caused someone else great pain and suffering; and then tell them how God was ever-present right in the middle of the mess that we had created for ourselves. Yet, that's exactly what this story is about.

I remember the exact day that God prompted me to write this book. I was about to start a week of prayer and fasting and I had just finished praying for God to lead me on the purposes of the fast. I was in the middle of making my bed, and just as simply as a parent tells a child to go do a chore, God spoke to my spirit and said, "write a book about the adultery." Of course, I argued back that there was no way I was sharing THAT part of my story with the whole world.

Well, if you know God like I do, you know that He doesn't let us get off the hook that easily. He always knows what is best for us and will certainly use our pain for His purposes. So, I chose to operate in obedience and allow God to prepare my heart for what I would consider to be one of the hardest assignments I have ever been given.

I wish I could say that I got started writing the book the very first day of my praying and fasting and was finished with it by the end of that year, but that's not true. This book has taken me on a journey of deep inner soul surrender that it has challenged every Truth I have ever claimed to believe.

I wish I could say that there was a miraculous healing in my heart and in my marriage prior to the writing of this book and that I am writing to encourage others to never give up hope, but there hasn't been a complete miracle. In fact, I still have hard days when I must persevere to find hope in the promises of God. The struggle comes less frequently these days, but I'm not exempt from it. Marriage is made up of 2 imperfect people who each bring their own set of circumstances. Marriage is hard.

The reality is that I am writing this book from a very exposed and honest place of struggle with my own will and emotions. I fight to stay married to my husband of 22 years. I fight the lies in my head that tell me that running away from all of it would be easier. I know that God wants me to stay married because He is bringing glory from the mess that we have made. I choose to walk in faith every single day, trusting that He is working in both of our hearts to bring forth a beautiful story of total restoration. But to say that I am completely 'in the clear' would not be true.

UNEXPECTED TRAGEDY

Since I began writing this book three years ago, we have endured even more trials and suffering. A year and a half into my writing this, we faced an unexpected tragedy of the worst kind. Our disabled daughter Anna passed away from a tragic accident. It was just one month after her 18th birthday and her decision to be baptized at church. She wasn't sick and it wasn't caused by any of her medical problems. We didn't see it coming at all, yet our entire way of life changed in one moment.

I plan to tell Anna's complete story in a future book, but I want to take a moment to briefly share a portion of it here.

Anna's life had been one battle after another to keep her healthy and alive. From day one, she faced challenges of every kind. It started with her being exposed to Group B Strep during her birth to a heart murmur, reflux, apnea, and seizure activity all within the first few weeks of life. She left the hospital at 21 days old prescribed with 5 different medications and under the care of 6 different specialists. She was eventually diagnosed with a rare genetic disorder known as Monosomy 1P36 Deletion syndrome.

Her lifelong care involved 6 major operations, countless hospital studies and stays, every type of therapy, many different medications, in-home caregivers, and a constant search for answers and treatments to improve her quality of life. She never walked. She never talked. She never fed herself, dressed herself, crawled, used the toilet, or gained any self-care abilities. She had severe scoliosis and grand mal seizures. She suffered constant UTI's. Her body was thin and frail, and weight gain was a constant struggle. And while her life was hard, she exuberated a joy about her that could have only come from the Lord.

I had always known that we wouldn't have Anna for a long time. She was simply on loan to me from above. In fact, doctors told us not to expect her to make it past 5 years old. So, we considered every day of her 6,607 days on this earth with us to be a gift from God. Sure, there were plenty of hard days that certainly didn't seem like 'gifts.' But some of my greatest moments of growth in my faith happened on those hard days.

"Dear brothers and sisters, when troubles of any kind come your way, consider it an opportunity for great joy. For you know that when your faith is tested, your endurance has a chance to grow. So let it grow, for when your endurance is fully developed, you will be perfect and complete, needing nothing."
James 1: 2-4 NLT

I believe there is a power greater than anything I've ever known working in our marriage and in our family right now for me to be able to be sitting at this keyboard writing a book about one trial that could have destroyed us while processing the grief from another. That power does not exist outside of the Holy Spirit's dwelling in me.

This endurance only grows stronger through faith. My faith in Jesus Christ alone is why I continue to write. If *just one person* can catch an understanding of this kind of faith, all of Heaven will rejoice. Faith sustains us. Faith strengthens us. Faith draws us into His presence. Faith is what we embrace in our surrender. And faith is why I continue to run this race called life with endurance.

Faith is what we embrace in our surrender. And faith is why I continue to run this race called life with endurance.

Anna was a beautiful child from God. While her life came with challenges that could bring an entire day's plans to a halt, the work that God did through her life encompasses my belief in His awesomeness. I had no idea that the baby who changed my entire future trajectory would also be the baby who saved my life from myself.

Nothing taught me surrender like my disabled child whose needs extended beyond my own human capabilities. Nothing taught me surrender like needing God so badly just to pick myself up off the floor one more time in the midst of endless discouraging reports. And when I was faced with the most devastating news a parent can receive, its only by surrender to God that my faith enabled me to stand strong instead of crumble.

Anna saved me from myself by forcing me to deal with the prideful attitude that I had developed in my early 20's. It was a season of my life when I decided to take my life's plans into my own hands. My attitude was that I was going to do what I wanted to do, and I didn't need direction from God, even though He was still orchestrating every step I made. Thankfully, it was a short season of my life!

My plans to finish my college degree and be a career mom were completely my own, not having consulted God about any of it. I believed that I was smart enough to be successful on my own without God's help. I decided that going to church would be reduced to just another item on the checklist of 'the right things to do' to be considered a good person. It was all show. It was shallow and superficial, and it wasn't being true to the little girl who had heard God speak to her spirit since she was just a child.

When Anna's life didn't fall into line with *my* plans, I was forced to alter my course to provide her with the care she needed. For a long time, I held a deep resentment about that sacrifice that I felt forced to make. Today, I know that God used Anna to interrupt the wrong direction that I was headed. He used her life to draw me back to Him. He used her circumstances to bring me back to utter dependence on His presence and His help.

Without her, I never would have come to know Him as intimately as I do now. I can envision the cold, bitter career woman that I would have been looming in the shadows of a life I was saved from. I'm thankful for His ways that are higher than my ways.

"My thoughts are not your thoughts," says the Lord. "And my ways are far beyond anything you could imagine. For just as the heavens are higher than the earth, so my ways are higher than your ways and my thoughts higher than your thoughts."
Isaiah 55: 9 NLT

The year that Anna died, I had chosen 'faith' as my word of the year. Each year, I choose a growth word and an accompanying scripture. The scripture for my word 'faith' was Hebrews 11:1.

"Now faith is the substance of things hoped for, the evidence of things not [yet] seen.
Hebrews 11:1 NKJV

I shared this scripture earlier in the book because it is such a powerful verse. If we can truly comprehend what faith like that looks like, we remove the barriers that hold us back from the abundant life promised to us. I got bold with my faith that year and decided to believe for Anna's complete healing.

When I picked that word and chose to believe for a huge miracle, I had no idea that my faith would be challenged with the hardest test I've ever faced. When Anna died, I knew that God was giving me the opportunity to grow substantially in my total faith in Him. I knew that my bold prayer had been answered, just differently than I had wanted and expected. Anna HAD been healed the moment she entered her eternal destination in Heaven. It didn't happen here on earth where I could see it, so I had to decide that I *fully* believed what I had professed in my scripture for the year.

My faith for Anna's healing was the *substance* of what I had hoped for. Her healing that happened when she arrived in Heaven was the *evidence* of what I couldn't yet see. God had solidified the words of Hebrews 11:1 in my spirit as my faith endured through all the stages of grief. Her whole life had been my training. Her death was my ultimate test of faith.

This brings me to the point in the story when I must share one of the most agonizing details of her death that was directly related to my marriage. It is not written to lay blame on anyone. I am simply truthfully telling the way it happened and sharing the feelings

I experienced to be as transparent as possible with how God worked through all of it. It is my belief that, if our marriage can survive *this*, then anyone reading this can trust God to save their marriage, too.

The summer that Anna died, Scott and I were attending a group marriage class at our church. The week just prior to her death, the topic we discussed hit a very deep nerve with an ongoing issue of constant frustration in our marriage. It was the topic of how each spouse may do things differently, but neither way is necessarily wrong just because it's different.

This topic immediately sparked a heated discussion between Scott and I regarding several things that we did differently when it came to the care of our kids, particularly Anna. In that discussion, I brought up how he had repeatedly disregarded the security measures I put in place to ensure Anna's safety in her daybed when she was tucked in at night. This involved safeguarding her from the possibility of an accidental strangulation in the iron bedframe by placing a large pillow between the frame and mattress above her head. It was the slightest possible accident that had never happened in the 5 years that she had slept in that bed. However, it was always a potential hazard in the back of my mind. I was always diligent to double-check on her before I went to bed each night. If Scott had neglected to take the steps to prevent this potential accident, I would tuck the pillow in place and then remind him of the importance of this safety protocol.

The weekend that followed that very significant marriage class discussion about Anna, I left on a girls' trip to Colorado with my daughter Sarah and some of our friends. Two days into our trip, I woke up to a text message from my son telling me that my husband had found Anna deceased in her bed that morning. I knew in that moment exactly what had happened without even being told. The one accident that I hoped would never happen had occurred while I was not there.

I can't begin to describe the wave of pain and devastation that rushed through my whole being with the words of that news. All I can tell you is that I hit the floor and cried out to God like I had never cried out before. I was blessed to be surrounded by the most wonderful sisters in Christ who began to pray fervently over Sarah and me. And God met me right there in that cabin in the mountains so far away from the devastation that had unfolded in my home. All the while, my husband and my son were forced to face it alone. Fortunately, a few of our wonderful men friends from church got to Scott shortly afterwards.

That fateful day had the potential to destroy our marriage and our family. It had the potential to destroy us, too. The nature of the accident itself was breeding ground for bitterness and unforgiveness. Many parents who face a loss like this never really recover. They move on because life forces us to move on, but they are never the same. But God!

It is only because God met me in my darkest hour of pain that I can write about it today. It is only because I hit my knees in desperate surrender to Him in my most devastating moment that I didn't succumb to the ways the world handles grief. All those years of surrendering were practice for that day when I didn't even know it. Daily surrender had taught me *exactly* where my help comes from!

"My help comes from the Lord, the Maker of Heaven and Earth."
Psalm 121:1 NIV

Just a few hours after I got the news, I boarded a plane back home, only to enter a life forever altered by a single incident. Yet, there was a peace over me with which God had covered me to walk through the next few days, weeks, and months to follow. I entered my home to a very broken and contrite husband who had endured his hardest moment as a parent without me. What he needed most in that moment was a wife whose faith in God's Word was stronger than whatever emotions were bubbling inside. You see, God tells me in Psalm 139 that He had numbered Anna's days on this earth before she was ever born.

"Every day of my life was recorded in your book. Every moment was laid out before a single day had passed."
Psalm 139: 16 NLT

God had given Anna life and God had called her home the exact day she was supposed to go home. God was in charge- not me, not Scott, nor her bedframe. Laying blame or holding resentment would not change what had happened. I knew that standing strong in my faith would bring glory to God even in our darkest hour. As a result,

I pressed into God's presence more so than I ever had in my life. I experienced God's peace that surpasses understanding in such a tangible way that I could say that I felt like He was carrying me. And He has continued to carry me through this journey of grief that I must walk every day.

> *There's one way that is a tried-and-true formula for not only surviving but thriving. That one thing is called FAITH.*

FAITH IT 'TIL YOU MAKE IT

The truth that I have learned throughout this journey from the adultery and now through the loss of our daughter is that only one thing will bring beauty from the ashes. Only one answer will get me through the hardest days. The façade won't sustain me when I feel like giving up. A fake smile and a fancy dress won't work for a broken heart and a wounded soul. No amount of faking it is going to make everything improve on its own. There's one way that is a tried-and-true formula for not only surviving but *thriving*. That one thing is called FAITH.

I can't fake it 'til I make it with grief. Grief must be felt and acknowledged to get to the other side. I can't spiritualize it or cover the pain with a bandage made from happy feel-good words. No, I must allow it to flow naturally from my heart and head into the loving arms of Father God. I must let Him hold me in my darkest hours and be authentic with my pain. Only then can He replace the tears of grief with the tears of joy. Only then can He replace the lies that linger in the back of my mind where blame and bitterness try to take root with the sovereign Truth of His Word.

I must tell myself that it's okay to admit to Him when I feel too weak to face another day. Those days tend to start the worst and end the best. Why? Because those are the days that He does His best work. Those are the days when surrender delivers a whole new level of power within me.

"Each time He [the Lord] said, "My grace is all you need. My power works best in weakness."
2 Corinthians 12: 9 NLT

I have learned that to fully admit my weaknesses in humble surrender to God actually *strengthens* my faith in His promises of healing and redemption. Surrender is an exchange between me and God. I give him my hurt and weakness, and He gives me His healing power and restoration.

"So now I am glad to boast about my weaknesses, so that the power of Christ can work through me. That's why I take pleasure in my weaknesses, and in the insult's, hardships, persecutions, and troubles that I suffer for Christ. For when I am weak, then I am strong."
2 Corinthians 12: 9b-10 NLT

The strength that comes from the power of Christ within us is *supernatural* strength. It does not exist in a life lived outside of God's will. There's no protein shake or physical workout program that can create the kind of strength in a person that can even begin to compare with the God-strength within someone.

Supernatural strength is not attained in a gym on fancy workout equipment or by an intense personal trainer. It's not physical at all. No, it's built deep inside our spiritual muscles when we exercise a face-down position in our prayer closet praying to God to meet us there in that secret place.

I give him my hurt and weakness, and He gives me His healing power and restoration.

I'm reminded of the way a butterfly emerges from a cocoon. It goes in as a fat little pudgy caterpillar with no ability to do anything except eat through leaves and crawl on its little legs. But something supernatural happens inside the secret place of that cocoon. No one on the outside can see what is happening inside. Only the caterpillar and its Creator have the privilege to experience the process of metamorphosis taking place inside. Then, one day, it finally breaks through the walls of the hard outer protective covering of the cocoon. Out into the open air bursts a beautiful butterfly with wings for flying and the strength to go high into the air. What happened in secret is now visible to the outside world.

We can be like the butterfly. The development and strengthening of our spiritual wings happen in the cocoon of our prayer life. It's that time when it's just us and God. It's when we stand naked and unashamed before Him with our hearts laid out to be examined and healed. No one sees us laboring in prayer before God on our face- no one but God- our Creator. And when we finally emerge, we have been changed into a stronger creation than the one who entered.

Supernatural strength is what people see in me when they tell me, "You're so strong. Knowing all that you've walked through, and you still have a smile on your face." In reality, I'm only as strong as God who lives in me. Without Him, I am so very human and weak. But with Him, people see His strength in me. They notice that it's different than the rest of the world. Because its supernatural, and it does not exist outside of a surrendered life in Him.

I'm only as strong as God who lives in me.

We didn't move out of our home after Anna died. I felt that moving away would be running from pain instead of confronting it. It would have been easier to sell our house and start fresh somewhere else. In fact, it was a seller's market at the time, and new houses in new neighborhoods were popping up everywhere. But we stayed in this home filled with memories of Anna. We had the opportunity to exercise our faith muscles right here in this home that held 12 years of life lived with Anna. We faced the new reality of life in our home without Anna one day at a time.

JOY COMES IN THE MO(U)RNING

"Though weeping may last through the night, but joy comes in the morning."
Psalm 30: 5 NLT

Every morning, I go into Anna's bedroom and open the blinds. Many times, I sit down on the floor in the spot where she most likely took her last breath. I pray in that spot and ask God to show me that Anna is now with Him. I have slept in her room many times, too. I pray for dreams about Anna that bring me so much comfort. I choose to never run away from the hardest things to face. Rather than close the door to her room to avoid facing the reality of her absence, we choose to see her room as the place she entered Heaven's gates.

I've rearranged the furniture since she died, and I replaced the bed. I gave away most of her clothes to a dear friend's little girls who send me pictures every time they wear one of her outfits and hairbows. Her room is full of toys for our grandchildren to enjoy when they visit. Many of those toys belonged to Anna. It's the most light and airy room in the house. It's full of life and full of joy. Happy memories of Anna reside in that room. Faith won and God's glory shines bright there.

Faith won and God's glory shines bright there.

It took a battle to get to this point- a battle that happened in my prayer time. It was won from the faith that emerged victoriously from that secret place with my Heavenly Father. I cried out to Him in that room many times. I asked Him the hard questions that had challenged my faith. I didn't back down and give up. As my faith wings grew stronger in that private time with Him, I got bold with how I walked through grief in the days and months that followed. I got so bold in my faith that I chose 'joy' as my word of the year for the following year.

"Do not grieve, for the joy of the Lord is your strength."
Nehemiah 8: 10 NIV

It turns out that grief and joy are two sides of the same coin. My very wise counselor taught me that. Without experiencing grief, we can never fully appreciate true joy. More than any other trial I went through in life, grief made me the hungriest for the joy of the Lord.

Choosing the word 'joy' would certainly stretch me. I had learned enough about God by then to know that His teaching me and growing me in my word of the year would most often look nothing like I planned. So, it shouldn't have surprised me when the year that I chose "joy," the entire world was forced into quarantine by an unfamiliar virus called COVID-19.

Just 8 months after the loss of Anna, the state of Texas, along with the rest of the nation, issued a stay-at-home order as a means of quarantine while the government scrambled to find a solution for the coronavirus.

I jokingly thought to myself during that time, "What a perfect setup for growing in joy this year!"

There's nothing like a stay-at-home order to force you to take a good hard look at your home life and your family and see exactly where the work needs to happen. There's no avoiding it when you can't leave. Those months that forced us to be at home brought much healing to our overall spiritual atmosphere. And there was certainly great opportunity for joy to be cultivated!

To understand joy, we must study the fuller, spiritual meaning. Joy is about *inner* contentment that isn't swayed by *external* situations. It's about coming to the understanding that God uses the hardest trials in our life to produce an endurance that brings us into the fullness of our purpose.

Rather than look at the trials as something meant to harm us, we learn to look at them as opportunities to develop patience and inner strength. Since inner strength comes only from God, our joy increases as we learn to rely on that inner strength more than on what is happening around us. We make it our *choice* to choose joy.

We make it our choice to choose joy.

Joy is a fruit of the Holy Spirit. When the Holy Spirit resides in us, joy is one of the products of His presence. When we choose a life led by His presence, we choose joy.

"But the Holy Spirit produces this kind of fruit in our lives: love, joy, peace, patience, kindness, goodness, faithfulness, gentleness, and self-control."
Galatians 5:22-23 NLT

During that quarantine when everything in our world was nothing like it had been, I discovered that joy truly had been manifested in me. Our home felt peaceful and pleasant. We enjoyed doing home improvement projects that we had been putting off. We made the changes to Anna's room. We watched church service online together in our living room. We spent time with the people we valued most. We embraced the simple life and slowed down long enough to appreciate the things we had taken for granted.

CHOOSING SURRENDER

I know without a doubt that choosing daily surrender prepared me in advance for everything that was going to come: the long-term effects of adultery, catastrophic loss, a virus that changed the way the world operated, and a heart that needed to recalibrate its navigation system.

My daily surrender to my Heavenly Father is bringing complete healing to my heart, soul, and marriage. I surrender wrong thought patterns to Him daily. I fight the thoughts from the enemy that play lies in my head and remind me of old hurts because I know that they are his attempts to keep me from reaching total freedom. God is bigger than every lie and every hurt- old or new. I cry out to God to help me stay joyful, and He reminds me that intimately knowing Him will always bring joy.

My daily surrender has been the key to placing life's priorities in the correct order. I've been able to see things through God's perspective. Surrender is essential for pruning the unnecessary things that take our attention off Him. My faith feels unshakable. I stand on the solid ground of God's Word. I choose joy when nothing around me appears joyful. And I walk with confidence and courage into whatever the future holds.

REFLECTION QUESTIONS:

- What do you need to surrender to get your priorities in the right order?

- Will you make an exchange with God today? Give Him you hurts and weaknesses in exchange for His healing power and restoration.
- Have you experienced any catastrophic events in your life that you can see where God carried you through it? Did your faith grow stronger?
- Are you willing to choose joy in whatever circumstances lie ahead?

☩ ☩ ☩

WALKING IN VICTORY

> *"If you don't know where you are going, any*
> *road will take you there." - Cheshire Cat*

A CROSSROADS MOMENT: VICTORY OR DEFEAT?

I want to start this final chapter with a quote made by the Cheshire Cat in Lewis Carroll's "Alice in Wonderland." The cat says to Alice, "If you don't know where you are going, any road will take you there."

There's a lot of truth packed into that single sentence spoken by the imaginary character in that beloved children's book. It most certainly compels us to consider our long-term goals as we decide how to move forward.

We make choices every single day: Where are we heading? Where do we want to go? Where will we end up? What is the final goal? These are our opportunities to exercise our power to select. They're also opportunities that challenge us to find a definitive answer. Otherwise, we will end up wandering aimlessly through life, walking through each day like a vagabond with no direction. It's an unsettling way to live. Without a planned destination, we won't have a goal to work towards and we can waste years focused on something that will not bear good fruit in our lives.

All seriousness aside for a second, I must confess something that happens to me more often than I would like to admit. Some days, I get in my car to head out for some errands or a lunch date. Oftentimes, I will back out of my garage, push the button to open my side mirrors, push the garage door button to close it, and drive away from the house. I get no more than just out of sight of the house and I will think to myself, "Did I close the garage door?" And I won't be able to remember if I just did it. So, I do a turnaround at the first "T" in the road and go back by my house to check if the garage door had been left open. Lo and behold, it is closed *every single time!* I let out a sigh of relief, slightly frustrated that I couldn't remember doing it in the first place, and I drive away again. Not a huge deal, I know. But it gets worse.

As I drive away for good, I will get distracted while putting on a song from my playlist or by stopping at the mailbox that I'll leave the neighborhood in the complete wrong direction for where I'm supposed to be going. This isn't a huge error to correct, thank goodness, but it still gets worse.

If I have farther than a couple of miles to drive, I have been known to get so preoccupied with passionately singing along to my music in the car that I get completely sidetracked from where I was headed in the first place. I've missed my exit altogether several times, forcing me to roam around the city streets until I get back on the path to where I was headed. This is no joke! It's embarrassing! And I'm usually alone when this has happened, so no one ever knew about it until just now. Whew- confession done!

I know I'm not the only one who has had this happen to them. I find an ounce of comfort in knowing that it's a common experience for other people. I feel a little less worried that there might be something seriously wrong with my brain function when I hear about someone else doing something similar. The good thing is that it has never led to any serious consequences. And I've never arrived late to something important because of it. If anything, it kept me from getting to my favorite shopping place as quickly as I wanted, which probably saved me some money by cutting down my available shopping time.

While this story makes me laugh as I type it out as a sort of confession, I'm also grateful that this hasn't been a regular occurrence in the way I navigate through my life. Sure, I've lost my way a few times. As a teenager and a young adult, I willingly exited the right path for a wild ride on the wrong one. And when I was blindsided by the deception of adultery, I certainly lost my way for a while as I roamed around the streets of sin city!

Well, praise God that He offered me another "T" in the road to turn around and double-check where the door to sin had been left open. I'm especially thankful that He gave me the chance to close the door for good by never forgetting what put me there in the first place.

As I write the final chapter of this book from where I stand today, I confess that I come to a familiar crossroads on my narrow road journey ever so often. It's the crossroads of victory or defeat. I stop at the stop sign and stare at the brilliant green signs that illuminate the two direction choices.

Some days are a no-brainer as I quickly turn onto Victory Road. Those are the good days. Those are the days when everything goes right from the moment I step out of bed and thank God for another blessed day. It's those days when God meets me right where I need Him, and nothing rattles my faith. It's those days when the sun shines bright, and the air is the perfect temperature. My kids are pleasant, and I'll go out on a limb here and say, they're even grateful for what I do as a mom. Scott and I work well together on those day. We may do a project on the house together or have a conversation that goes well. Even my dogs behave well on those days, LOL.

Everything I just described is the external things going the way I believe they should go. They're mostly easy. Victory feels easy because there isn't really a battle to face.

But what happens on days that feel like total defeat? I have an occasional one of those, too. Those are the days that truly earn the title of 'Victory Road,' and I'll tell you why. Those are the days when an actual victory is accomplished through operating in faith and joy. Those are the days when I must face every single hardship *from* a place of victory *before* I reach the outcome.

> *Fighting from victory means standing strong in the certainty of God's already finished work on the cross.*

I hope you caught that- fighting *from* victory, not *for* it. Fighting *from* victory means standing strong in the certainty of God's already finished work on the cross. It means activating my faith by *spiritually* seeing victory even when I can't *physically see* it. Remember Hebrews 11:1 NIV? "Faith is the *evidence* of what we can't yet see." Faith in these moments may look bizarre to people on the outside. It's like saying we are winning a war when we just lost an entire military regiment to an explosive bomb.

I want to invite you into a glimpse of what it looks like on a day that could easily be described as a defeat day. A day like this typically starts with me waking up with a massive headache that forces me out of bed and to the kitchen for some ibuprofen. Then, I sit in the dark on my sofa with heating pads on my neck and head, praying for God to take away this headache. If it goes away, I will have usually lost several hours from my morning. My time alone with God consisted of nothing more than praying for relief, and no time reading my Bible or journaling.

As I try to make up for lost time, there will usually be some upset from one of my kids that feels like an attack on my identity as a mother. After that, it never fails that a dog will either vomit or use the bathroom on the living room rug or make some other mess that I must clean up.

At some point in the day, I may find myself on the receiving end of some insecure person's passive-aggressive actions, or someone seems to get angry at me for no apparent reason. I'll manage to get through the day without accomplishing a single task, except make the bed, if I didn't crawl back into it.

That evening, Scott will come home stressed from work, and it will be the day that a hot topic erupts into argument. Forget dinner because I'll just order food. And someone will complain that I never cook anymore. After dinner is just a blur because I simply want to crash in bed and hide from everyone, including the dogs. Eventually, my day comes to an end. I lie in bed too tired to pray for anything substantial, except to beg God that tomorrow will be better, and I fall asleep. Sounds terrible, right?

Honestly, I have had hard days just like I described above that cause me to completely give over to defeat by lunchtime. Those days do not end well.

Just the same, I've had other hard days that I persevere to stay in a position of victory *despite* the difficult circumstances. My determination to maintain a victorious attitude becomes so strong that I start to challenge Satan to bring it on! The more things that hit me and try to knock me down, the faster I stand back up and say, "not today!" Joy overrides the upsets, and victory takes it stand. Nothing changed in the external, but everything changed in the internal. It was all about how I responded. THAT'S the road to victory!

EXERCISING THE COURAGE MUSCLES

It takes practice to stay on the road to victory on the days that feel like defeat. It's the same way an athlete practices and exercises to get better and stronger every day. The athlete has a prize in mind. They want to win the game when they face their opponent. They want to beat their personal best record. They want to break a world record. They want to overcome a barrier to a skill or remove a mental block. Something motivates them to push themselves harder and further. There is a goal at the end of their road to victory. There will be defeat along the way, but the athlete must stay focused on the goal.

"Don't you realize that in a race everyone runs, but only one person gets the prize? So run to win! All athletes are disciplined in their training. They do it to win a prize that will fade away, but we do it for an eternal prize. So I run with purpose in every step."
1 Corinthians 9:24-256 NLT

What is your goal? Ask yourself why you felt led to buy this book and read it. Something motivated you to read it to the end. Something kept you committed to it even when it might have struck a nerve in you that you didn't like. Something spoke to you in a way that you could identify and made you hope for a positive outcome. You stuck with me this far because you want victory in your own life.

Your struggle may not be marriage-related at all. That's okay. I truly believe that adultery is like other sins in the sense that it is a symptom that stems from a deeper root cause. Maybe you're not struggling with a sin temptation at all. That's okay, too. You may be simply looking for a deeper authentic connection to God because your soul needs reviving. My prayer for this book is that anyone who reads it can find their own personal victory from the one true source of help- our Heavenly Father who just really loves us.

Long before I wrote this book, I read many books about marriage, marital problems, adultery, betrayal, and just self-help in general. I had goals for my marriage as much as I had goals for my life. I never *wanted* to commit adultery. It certainly wasn't a goal for something like that to become part of our story. But over and above that, I never would have wanted to experience the near-death of my soul that I ended up facing as a consequence for my sin. Looking back, I can honestly say that it took something as bad as adultery to serve as my wake-up call that I had a very broken soul that needed to get real before God. Just proof that God uses all things for good.

> *"And we know that God causes everything to work together for the good of those who love God and are called according to his purpose for them."*
> *Romans 8: 28 NLT*

I love this verse. It is a confirmation to my soul that God used my sin of adultery to compel me to seek deep spiritual healing and to return to a life-giving relationship with Him. He loved me enough NOT to leave me there. And I loved Him enough to be receptive to His correction and His calling me back to Him.

> *"For God knew his people in advance, and he chose them to become like his Son, so that his Son would be the firstborn among many brothers and sisters. And having chosen them, he called them to come to him. And having called them, he gave them right standing with himself. And having given them right standing, he gave them his glory."*
> *Romans 8: 29-30 NLT*

God is calling you to Him, too! He will never leave you stuck in your mess if you are willing to acknowledge it, deal with it, and leave it behind as you walk into the fullness of His presence. He won't stop loving you. He didn't stop loving me. He promises us that victory is still ours if we will just take hold of it.

"Can anything ever separate us from Christ's love? Does it mean he no longer loves us if we have trouble or calamity, or are persecuted, or hungry, or destitute, or in danger, or threatened with death? (As the Scriptures say, "For your sake we are killed every day; we are being slaughtered like sheep.") No, despite all these things, overwhelming victory is ours through Christ, who loved us."
Romans 8:35-37 NLT

He will never leave you stuck in your mess if you are willing to acknowledge it, deal with it, and leave it behind as you walk into the fullness of His presence.

When Anna died, it didn't mean that God didn't love me anymore, so He let it happen. Romans 8:35 assures me that her death had nothing to do with His love for me. Also, it's not because He doesn't love us when we face a defeating day.

With that being said, I DO think that *some* troubles could be avoided by turning away from sin as fast as we can. Some of our troubles are most definitely self-inflicted.

I write about God's unfailing love with a warning, though. God will ALWAYS love us, for certain. But we must repent of our sins. I said it before, and I'll say it again. I stress this truth repeatedly throughout the book because it is a pivotal step towards redemption. His love and grace are not a license to keep sinning. We have a responsive part to play in it. We must repent and live God's way.

"And athletes cannot win the prize unless they follow the rules."
2 Timothy 2: 5 NLT

I remind you that repentance is the action of changing our mind about sin. By changing our mind, we depend on God to help us turn away from sin and turn towards Him. Repentance is a step towards victory. It's the first workout to begin with when we are strengthening our faith muscles.

Each time we repent, we are training our mind to turn away from a sin or temptation and we are exercising the muscles that make us stronger for the next time. And the next time. And the time after that. The temptation to sin won't ever go away as long as we are alive on this planet. But our ability to walk in victory over the temptation will grow stronger every time we depend on God to exercise our resistance. And the Holy Spirit's strength within us increases as the temptation's power decreases.

> *Each time we repent, we are training our mind to turn away from a sin or temptation and we are exercising the muscles that make us stronger for the next time. And the next time. And the time after that.*

It takes courage to openly admit our weaknesses to someone who can hold us accountable. God tells us to confess to one another. I recommend joining a small group or going to a licensed professional counselor. I do both of these things. Accountability is a good thing because we shed light on something that used to be hidden in darkness when we confess it to another believer. And another believer may be able to see something in us that we are unable to see about ourselves. A trusted confidant is a valuable gift!

"Confess your sins to each other and pray for each other so that you may be healed. The earnest prayer of a righteous person has great power and produces wonderful results."
James 5: 16 NLT

My word the year I finished writing this book was 'courage.' I chose courage because I needed to face every inhibition that I had about writing it. I couldn't be afraid of what people might think of me by knowing all of this. I had to focus on the goal of victory that God showed me was already mine. I had to focus on how telling the truth would help other people face their own hard truths. I knew that this story was no longer just about *me*. The victory is so much bigger than my own personal goal now. God wants to move in the hearts of His people. I believe He wants to use my testimony and *your* testimony to help someone else.

"Here's another way to put it: You're here to be light, bringing out the God-colors in the world. God is not a secret to be kept. We're going public with this, as public as a city on a hill. If I make you light-bearers, you don't think I'm going to hide you under a bucket, do you? I'm putting you on a light stand. Now that I've put you there on a hilltop, on a light stand—shine! Keep open house; be generous with your lives. By opening up to others, you'll prompt people to open up with God, this generous Father in heaven."
Matthew 5:14-16 MSG

When I face a hard day in the present time, the goal of victory helps me keep moving forward. Trust me, I battle the feelings of wanting to give up from time to time. But someone's salvation decision may be on the other side of my obedience. If I take my eyes off the prize of eternity in Heaven, I will most certainly become defeated.

"I don't know about you, but I'm running hard for the finish line. I'm giving it everything I've got. No lazy living for me! I'm staying alert and in top condition. I'm not going to get caught napping, telling everyone else all about it and then missing out myself."
1 Corinthians 9:26-27 MSG

Exercising our courage muscles by being vulnerable to a trusted friend or counselor takes humility. We can't walk through life acting like we have it all together all the time and then be surprised when the bottom falls out from under us.

We can't walk through life acting like we have it all together all the time and then be surprised when the bottom falls out from under us.

We must also possess the humility to accept the wisdom and correction from another person, even when we want to disagree with the hard truth that they speak to us. Remaining teachable is important for growth.

God puts us in community for a reason. We can be certain of the fact that we will play the role of both giver of grace and recipient of grace in our lifetime. We give and we get. We have a responsibility on both sides of that exchange.

"My dear brothers and sister, if someone among you wanders away from the truth and is brought back, you can be sure that whoever brings the sinner back from wandering will save that person from death and bring about the forgiveness of many sins."
James 5: 19-20 NLT

Victory belongs to us if we will just take hold of it. There are the small daily victories, the larger victories over a reoccurring struggle, and the final victory over death itself. Eternity waits for our arrival in Heaven. Heaven is the ultimate prize for this race we run called life. Heaven is our final victory.

SPEAKING LIFE

Walking in victory also involves the way we speak about our circumstances. Whining and complaining is detrimental to being victorious. Trust me, I like to complain just as much as the next person. Get me started on a soapbox of my problems, and I can saturate you in my sorrow. But I regret it every time I sink to that level of defeat. It serves no purpose for growth, and it brings other people down with it. Our words have power. Every time we speak, we are activating something negative or positive in the spiritual realm.

"Death and life are in the power of the tongue, and those who love it will eat its fruit."
Proverbs 18:21 NKJV

A power-packed verse of truth right there! God speaks about the power of our tongue a lot in the Bible. Anytime He talks about something often, I take that as a sign that it's very important.

> *Every time we speak, we are activating something negative or positive in the spiritual realm.*

When I feel tempted to speak deadly words about my marriage, I must learn to be silent. This is exactly the spot that I find myself in the most, these days. I'm learning to hold my tongue when the soapbox speech starts to bubble up to my mouth, being slow to speak.

"Everyone should be quick to listen, slow to speak and slow to become angry, because human anger does not produce the righteousness that God desires."
James 1: 19-20 NIV

Learning to control that tongue takes practice and dedication. It's another part of the exercise routine. As the self-control muscles get stronger, my tongue won't be as likely to blurt out negative things. I practice speaking positive words that give life. It doesn't just come naturally. But it's getting easier the more I do it. I don't beat myself up when I have a setback, either. Every small victory is a step in the right direction.

THINGS I'VE LEARNED ALONG THE WAY

I want to end this book with a list of important truths for you to keep in your pocket. This list would be much longer if I were to include every single thing that I choose to believe as an important part of running my race towards victory. I'll just sum it up to a few of the key points. I encourage you to make your own list, too. Your race with God is in your own lane. I'll be running beside you, cheering you on from *my* lane. I may never meet you face-to-face, but we will celebrate our victories together in Heaven, one day.

I think that the number one truth on the list deserves a whole paragraph rather than just a bullet point. This truth is that we ALL need Jesus Christ! We need to repent and receive the gift of salvation that only comes from Him. He paid the price for us when He died for our sins on that cross. Nothing else on this list matters if we don't fully grasp this Truth first and foremost.

If you have never asked Jesus Christ to be your Lord and Savior and to forgive you of your sins, I encourage you to stop reading and proclaim your need for a personal relationship with Him right now! Don't just say a repeated prayer that you've most likely heard recited in church on a regular basis. I could give you the words for your prayer, but I'm not going to do that. He's not looking for any formal prayer, anyways. He wants you to talk to Him in your own way.

I want you to get down on your knees and pray the words from your own heart and soul. Tell the Lord that you need Him. Seek forgiveness. Truly repent of your sins. Listen for what God is prompting you to say. He wants you to talk to Him like a Father. Take your time with this. Just talk to Him as long as you need.

He wants to hear your own heartfelt words of confession and repentance. He is waiting for you to make a commitment to Him in your own personal way. This truth is the gamechanger for the rest of your life. Don't take it lightly and don't skip over it! Without Jesus, we have nothing!

PAUSE AND PRAY!

Now that you've invited Jesus to be your Lord and Savior, don't expect life to get magically easy. It will most certainly have plenty of more trials to overcome. The difference is that you have a Helper who will never leave your side. I have learned that this is a fact. Along with that truth, I leave you with the rest of my list.

I have learned that:

1. We need Jesus first and foremost.
2. There's no magical moment of 'arrival.'
3. Peace will only come from total surrender.
4. Obedience is everything- be a doer of the Word.
5. If you wait to do your part until you are 'qualified', you will never feel qualified to accomplish your purpose.
6. You were born for a specific purpose that only YOU can fulfill at this time in eternity.
7. If you allow your mistakes and poor choices to dictate your destiny, you will experience a deep spiritual regret.
8. There are people on this planet whose salvation will come from your obedience and sensitivity to the Holy Spirit.
9. If you choose to ignore God's calling, He will use another to accomplish His will.
10. Freedom is available to everyone.
11. It's not always easy, but it's worth it.

IT'S NOT ALWAYS EASY, BUT IT'S WORTH IT

Dear friend, I pray that I have encouraged you to find freedom in your own life. I pray that you will trust God Almighty with your entire soul. Hide nothing from Him. Be a doer of His Word, even when it's not easy. Obedience is a wonderful thing. Let this book be your call to action.

"But don't just listen to God's Word. You must do what it says. Otherwise, you are only fooling yourselves. For if you listen to the Word and don't obey it, it is like glancing at your face in a mirror. You see yourself, walk away, and forget what you look like. But if you look carefully into the perfect

*law that sets you free, and if you do what it says and don't
forget what you heard, then God will bless you for doing it."
James 1:22-25 NLT*

I write this book for every person who has been where I've
been. I write it for the person who may be currently entangled in an
adulterous affair, for the person who may be entertaining the thought
of entering any form of infidelity, and for the person whose journey is
completely different from this, altogether. I pray that the transparency
of my heart be heard, and that the Truth of God's Word be received.
God promises that He is near the broken hearted. He will not leave
you nor forsake you. He will help you overcome every battle you face
if you allow Him. I don't promise that it will be easy. It hasn't been
easy for me. But I DO promise that it will be worth it!

END NOTE

While I have emphasized the fact that marriage is a lifelong commitment, I would like to say to anyone who is experiencing an abusive situation in their marriage, please seek professional help and counseling for your situation. I do not support remaining in an abusive situation for any reason. When I speak of the lifelong commitment of marriage, it is in the context of a *safe* marriage.

Made in the USA
Coppell, TX
08 September 2023

21367114R10097